How to
Behave

THOMAS LOW NICHOLS

AMBERLEY

First edition published 1873

This edition first published 2015

Amberley Publishing
The Hill, Stroud
Gloucestershire, GL5 4EP
www.amberley-books.com

British Library Cataloguing in Publication Data.
A catalogue record for this book is available from the British Library.

ISBN 978 1 4456 4425 7 (print)
ISBN 978 1 4456 4438 7 (ebook)

Typesetting and Origination by Amberley Publishing.
Printed in the UK.

CONTENTS

Foreword	4
Preface	6
Introduction	8
Care of the Person	18
Clothes	24
Deportment	33
Manners	40
Accomplishments	46
Society	53
Etiquette	62
Conversation	72
The Family	89
Love	97
Marriage	105
Work	113
Service	120
Trade	125
Speculation	131
Professions	135
Aristocracy	144
Religion	149
Miscellaneous Maxims	152

FOREWORD

We all like to know our place, and none have ever been (or indeed ever will be) so keen than our Victorian ancestors. The etiquette of the day is always founded on the principles of common sense and easing embarrassment, and rather than shun these ideas altogether, as so many people today do, we should be more willing to learn what has gone before us in order to enhance our current lives and mores.

Sadly, many of our contemporaries will be thankful that the rules, edicts and strictures outlined in Nichols's book are no longer gospel in today's über-liberal and relaxed age. They fail to see that any society, from whatever era, always responds better to conventions and boundaries and flourish because of them.

There are too many examples in this book of codes that, although now largely abandoned, remain correct. The hat protocol that Nichol's prescribes is still *de rigueur* – it is just that few of us wear hats anymore, let alone doff them when passing an acquaintance in the street out of respect to other people.

Although we have dropped many of the manners listed in this book, there are times when Nichols was clearly ahead of the trend; he writes in a very uncharacteristic fashion about parents openly and outwardly *loving* their children – a habit the Victorians very rarely displayed, especially the aspirational classes at which his work will have been aimed.

This book can be read in two ways. On face value it can be enjoyed simply as a jolly jaunt to see how superficially different we are from those who have gone before us. But those who scratch the surface and delve deeper will realise the huge similarities between the Victorians and us now. Although it is a dirty concept to admit it publically, we still want to get things right and put our best foot forward – we just don't know how. But the Victorians did!

William Hanson
Etiquette Consultant, Author & Broadcaster
February 2015

www.williamhanson.co.uk

PREFACE

The number of Manners books, books of Etiquette, and Guides to Politeness and the Usages of Good Society, shows the want felt for instruction in good behaviour, and what have been called the minor morals. The supply has been in some proportion to the demand, and the demand shows a very laudable desire for improvement in the deportment, graces, and accomplishments which give a charm to society.

I have added to the number of these useful books, because those I have examined, however correct and admirable they may be in laying down rules of conduct, or laws of etiquette, do not generally appear to give the principles of social rights and duties, which are the basis of good behaviour. They seem to me rather external and superficial; whereas good manners are based on morals, and good intention must be the spring of all right action.

I have wished, also, to widen the scope of such instruction. Good behaviour is something more than the proper manners of the drawing room, the dinner; or the ball. It belongs to all our relations to and intercourse with each other; therefore I have treated of the relations of husbands and wives, parents and children, masters and servants, employers and employed, landlords and tenants, tradesmen and customers, lawyers and clients, physicians and patients, clergymen and parishioners; of the varied relations of men and women to each other in our complex civilisation, the mutual duties involved in those relations, and the kind of behaviour to each other which will best promote the welfare and happiness of the whole community, as well as the grace and excellence, the charm and enjoyment of what is called society.

I have tried to make a good and useful book, and I shall be very glad if I have succeeded in making one which will prove also interesting and agreeable to its, I hope, numerous readers – one worthy to take its place in a list of 'Works on Sanitary and Social Science'.

T. L. Nichols, November 1873

INTRODUCTION

Some time ago I wrote a little book which sold for sixpence, entitled *How to Live on Sixpence a Day*; showing that simple, pure, and very economical food is better for everybody than the most costly viands, and what are esteemed the greatest luxuries. I followed this with a larger one, *How to Cook* – partly original, partly a compilation of recipes – to show how well people can live at a very cheap rate, and at how slight a cost they can have a varied, abundant, and delicious diet. Now I finish the series with a still larger and more widely important work, on manners and morals, or the conduct of life, which I shall call *How to Behave*.

It is not merely a manners book – not simply a book of etiquette; but it treats of the elements of good manners, and the moral principles which are the basis of all right being and right doing of good behaviour. It is an attempt to teach, in the plainest and most thorough manner, what every man and woman ought to know and do for themselves, and their own health, comfort, dignity, and happiness, and in order that they may promote the comfort and happiness of all around them.

It is what we are, and thereby what we do, that gives us our value as members of society. In *Human Physiology, the Basis of Sanitary and Social Science*, I have said,

All our faculties are social. Our intellect demands conversation, appreciation, admiration. Reading and writing, or correspondence, are partial substitutes, but what we enjoy much more is the animation of the living voice, the fire of the eye, the quick explanatory movements of the features, all the charm of refined and intelligent companionship. Our mirth is social; our wit is wasted if we speak it not; our poetry must have hearers and readers; we make pictures and statues that they may be seen and enjoyed; our ambition, hope, pride, love of approbation, all refer to others – are social passions all. Our benevolence finds its objects in the world around us; our conscience, or sense of justice and right, regards our relations to our fellow-men. In these relations is our true life, our real happiness, and love to God finds its practical manifestation in love to our fellow-men. Chiefly and best, we love Him in nature and in man. Reason and Religion are here in perfect harmony.

Whenever people are brought into near relations and close contact with each other, their manners become of more importance, if possible, than what we call their morals, since a man may be very honest and well disposed, yet very disagreeable. To associate with others, people must be neat and clean, must have no repulsive and disgusting habits, and be kind, civil, obliging, and courteous in their behaviour to each other. Crabbed, snarling, complaining, rude, disputatious people are nuisances in any society. The essence of politeness is unselfishness, a sense of justice, a constant, habitual regard for the rights of others, and the discipline and habit of attention to the welfare, the convenience, and happiness of those around us, and all with whom we come into contact or proximity. Children from their earliest years should be trained to an unselfish consideration for the pleasure of others; and taught the delight of doing good. In all schools, civil, deferent, polite, conciliating, and obliging manners should be as carefully taught as the rudiments of learning. Manners really influence the character. Our thoughts and feelings are moulded by our actions.

I have quoted myself to show the animus of the book I am writing, and that I esteem it a very important part of the work of social reformation I have endeavoured to promote in all my writings, and especially in the book from which I have made the above extracts. But I shall now quote more freely from the writings of others, to show that I am not alone in my view of the importance of good manners to man and to society.

Burke wrote,

> Manners are of more importance than laws. In a great measure
> the laws depend on them. The law teaches us but here and
> there, and now and then. Manners are what vex or soothe,
> corrupt or purify, exalt or debase, barbarise or refine us, by
> a constant, steady, uniform, insensible operation, like that of
> the air we breathe. They give their whole colour to our lives.
> According to their quality, they aid morals, they supply them,
> or they totally destroy them.

My countryman, President Jefferson, writing from Paris in
1785, says,

> With respect to polite manners, without sacrificing too much
> the sincerity of language, I would wish my countrymen to
> adopt just so much of European politeness as to be ready to
> make all those little sacrifices of self which render European
> manners amiable, and relieve society from the disagreeable
> scenes to which rudeness often subjects it. Here, it seems that
> a man might pass a life without encountering a single rudeness.
> In the pleasures of the table they are far before us, because with
> good taste they unite temperance. I have never yet seen a man
> drunk in France, even among the lowest of the people.

My own experience, almost a century later, agrees mainly
with that of Mr Jefferson. There is a greater consumption of
brandy and absinthe in France than formerly, but still, one
may travel across France, or live for weeks in Paris without
ever seeing a Frenchman intoxicated. However cheap and
abundant wines and liquors may be, most Frenchmen have
too much *amour propre*, too much self-respect, too much
regard for the good opinion of others, to get drunk. And it is
delightful to live in a country where you are never intruded
upon, never crowded, never insulted; where the manners of
the whole people, from the highest to the lowest, are civil,
deferent, and obliging.

But even in England, where good manners are less cultivated,
there is a quick appreciation, and ready imitation of civility.
Dr Caldwell, an American physician, whose autobiography

was published in 1855, was in London in 1821, when some young American friends of his complained of the rudeness and neglect which they received from persons to whom they spoke in the streets. He told them the fault was probably in the bluntness of their own manners, and proposed that, for a small wager, they should try the experiment of walking about for some hours, while he asked questions of any persons they should designate. He says,

> I put questions to more than twenty persons of every rank, from the high-bred gentleman to the servant in livery, and received, in every such instance, a courteous, and, in most instances, a satisfactory reply. What seemed most to surprise my friends was, that the individual accosted by me almost uniformly imitated my own manner. If I uncovered, as I usually did to a gentleman, or even to a man of ordinary appearance and breeding, he did the same; and when I touched my hat to a liveried coachman or footman, his hat was immediately under his arm. So much may be done, and such advantages gained, by simply avoiding coarseness and vulgarity, and being wellbred and agreeable.

Mr Emerson, to continue my American quotations, says,

> Manners are the happy ways of doing things; each one a stroke of genius or of love, now repeated and hardened into usage. They form at last a rich varnish, with which the routine of life is washed, and its details adorned. If they are superficial, so are the dewdrops which give such a depth to the morning meadows. Manners are very communicable; men catch them from each other.
>
> Consuelo boasts of the lessons she had given the nobles in manners, on the stage and in real life. Talma taught Napoleon the art of behaviour. Genius invents fine manners, which the baron and the baroness copy very fast, and, by the advantage of a palace, better the instruction. They stereotype the lesson they have learned into a mode. The power of manner is incessant – an element as inconcealable as fire. The nobility cannot in any country be disguised, and no more in a republic or a democracy than in a kingdom. No man can resist their influence. There

are certain manners which are learned in good society of that force, that, if a person have them, he or she must be considered, and is everywhere welcome, though without beauty, or wealth, or genius. Give a boy address and accomplishments, and you give him the mastery of palaces, and fortunes where he goes; he has not the trouble of earning or owning them; they solicit him to enter and possess.

Lord Chesterfield cites the example of Lord Albemarle, who, without birth, estate, learning, or abilities, became colonel in the guards, governor of Virginia, groom of the Stole, and ambassador to Paris – appointments worth sixteen or seventeen thousand pounds a year. Lord Chesterfield said,

> Many people wondered, but I do not. It was his air, his address, his manner, and his graces. He pleased, and by pleasing, became a favourite; and by becoming a favourite became all that he has been since.

A finer example of the power of manner is found in the life of Count Rumford – a poor boy in Massachusetts, who founded the Royal Institution of Great Britain, and for many years governed the Kingdom of Bavaria. The fascination of his manner charmed all who knew him, and enabled him to carry out the most important philanthropic enterprises, of some of which I have given a brief account in *Count Rumford: How He Banished Beggary from Bavaria*.

Within my memory, the standard of manners in England and America has visibly declined. Thus we hear of 'gentlemen of the old school'. I fear that America, after a century of progress, could scarcely show many gentlemen like George Washington, or Thomas Jefferson. In England, the manners of the upper classes are more simple, and their morals better in some particulars than they were fifty years ago; but I judge that the manners, at least of the lower classes, have deteriorated; for the aged are more respectful than the young, and there are many complaints of the increase of the rough element in the population of towns, with its vulgarity, insolence, and brutality.

But England has undertaken the education of the whole people, and it is to be hoped that the young of all classes will be taught good manners and pure morals, as well as reading, writing, and arithmetic. To aid in this most needful and beneficent work, I write this little book, which I mean to make so clear, so plain, so adapted to the simple common sense of every reader, that its instructions shall be perfectly understood – a way 'so plain that the wayfaring man, though a fool, need not err therein.' It is not a sort of book that is likely to give one a reputation for literature or science – it is not likely to be reviewed in the quarterly, or even the weekly, magazines of criticism. But I hope it will do good. Bad manners stand in the way of all improvement in social organisation and conditions. They are a terror and a nuisance. They hinder co-operation, and they increase social divisions, and intensify class distinctions. A reform in manners must precede any beneficial reforms in politics and society. Once manners are truly reformed, all other reforms become less difficult.

How to behave is a matter of universal interest and utility. Every man, woman, and child, ought to know how to dress, act, converse, and respond to the varied demands of our social relations, in the best possible manner. Our whole life and society need reforming, educating, refining, and polishing, to bring out their highest use and beauty. Life is made up of little things; little acts, little courtesies, little enjoyments. He who does best in these, gives most pleasure to others, and secures most happiness to himself.

Do not say these things are trifles and of no importance. It is worth every man's study and effort to be a gentleman; and every woman should try to be a lady, in all that constitutes genuine ladyhood. All those things which combine to form the manners and guide the deportment of the lady and the gentleman are elements of human happiness. Happiness is the one object of all our hopes and efforts; and we must find it in the most perfect being and doing of which we are capable. It is the satisfaction of our highest faculties and aspirations. It comes in living our true life, and doing the very best we can for ourselves, which we can only do by promoting the welfare and happiness of our fellow creatures. It is the social law that we can be happy only by contributing to the happiness of others. The command to love our neighbour as ourselves is therefore a command to secure our own happiness; and there is no law of life which it is not our highest good and greatest happiness to obey. This is the basis of all justice and all morality. God commands, nature requires, only what is best for us and for all. There can be no right to do wrong. A true freedom is the right to do right.

Life consists in being and doing. The being comes from the constitution of the being; and the being is perfected, in its true development, by all genuine doing. The being of a man is the assemblage of all his capabilities. His bones and muscles, his strength and activity, his grace and beauty, his senses and organs, his propensities, sentiments, and intellectual faculties, all swell the wealth of his being. Each faculty has its own life, its own rights, and its own capabilities of happiness; and all combine to make up the harmony of the complete being, which we call a man; and it is the full, equal, and harmonious satisfaction of all these faculties, which constitutes the greatest happiness, and so fulfils the end of manhood. Low enjoyments come from the exercise of low faculties, separated from, or uncontrolled by higher. High enjoyments consist in the exercise of the noblest faculties of honour, devotion, benevolence, and justice. Nothing can fully satisfy the aspirations of the human soul, but the complete and harmonious gratification of all its desires and capabilities of enjoyment. Therefore, small things are of great consequence. A leaf is a little thing, but leaves make up the foliage of a tree, and each leaf has its own vital function. The little graces, accomplishments, and suavities of life, are like the leaves of the tree, like the petals of its flowers, like the thousand of minutes but charming things in nature which make up the sum of her attractions.

The happiness of life in the aggregate – of the lives of the millions of men, women, and children around us – is far more influenced by manners and behaviour; by the minor morals, or a regard to small rights and decorums; by kindness, politeness, and the elegancies of what some may think trifling accomplishments, than by noble or heroic actions of benevolence, or self-sacrifice, or magnanimity. Such acts fall within the opportunities of few, and cannot occur often; but the others may enter into our daily and hourly lives, and diffuse their influence over our whole existence; and this joy of being and action is radiated and reflected everywhere; and its circling blessings, like the light of the stars, spread through the universe.

Is it not a happiness to feel yourself charming; beautiful in form and feature, if so blessed; beautiful in carriage and manner; beautiful in the neatness and elegance of your dress; beautiful in the kindness and politeness that shine forth in every expression? You are happy in all this; you see others happy in admiring you. You feel that you add to the sum of human happiness. You are a living joy – a blessing in yourself, a blessing to all who see you. Men pause in their busiest walks to look at you, and feel better for the looking. Each visit you make diffuses a new joy. The day is full of delights. You give a new charm to many lives; thus happiness is radiated upon other spirits, and so on, outward and onward, until your beauty has charmed the world, and your smile, like the beams of those far-off stars, whose light has not yet reached us, will shine upon posterity.

And everything which contributes to the harmony of life in any being – every line of beauty, or motion of grace, or assemblage of pleasant colours, or concord of sweet sounds, is a real blessing; and every look, or word, or action, which gives pleasure and promotes happiness, becomes a high moral duty. This is no mere question of fancy, of caprice, of arbitrary custom, or fashion; but it is one of rights and duties, important enough for pulpits, and grave enough for legislators.

There is no rule of life which is not based on science, and which may not be referred to some principle or law. Doubtless there may be observances of etiquette which seem purely arbitrary and capricious, but they are few and of little consequence. Even these, if carefully examined, may be found to have, or to have had, some good reason. But every genuine and valuable rule of behaviour may be referred to some principle of natural law; so that the observance of what may seem at first glance a matter of trifling etiquette, may be a moral duty; and a breach of decorum a crime.

A rudeness to any person is an offence, and is even recognised as such in law. The neglect of politeness, in certain cases, is a positive rudeness. The man who does not do what is becoming to a gentleman, commits a sin of omission, which may be a very grave one. He who does not prevent an injury, when it is in his power, might almost as well inflict it. The man who neglects to save life is not much better than a downright murderer. So, a neglect of politeness may be the severest insult that can be offered.

Every breach of good manners is some violation of right.
very neglect of politeness is a failure in duty. Men and women
re members of society, and have social wants and social
duties growing out of their social relations. It is not enough
that we let people alone, and injure no one. It is not enough
to 'cease to do evil'; we must also 'learn to do well'. Every
faculty and every organ has its own special rights – the right
not to be offended; the right to gratification and pleasure.
Taste has the right not to be compelled to eat unsavoury
food; and the right to seek for gustatory enjoyments. The
parent who compels a child to eat food which is loathsome
to its unperverted taste, violates the rights of this sense. The
host who provides good food, and the cook who prepares
it, exercise the politeness of taste, and satisfy the rights of
appetite. The smell has its rights, but they are everywhere
violated. Whoever fills the air I must breathe with unpleasant
odours, is guilty of a wrong. If the smell is merely unpleasant,
it is an impoliteness; if unwholesome, it is a crime; and, as a
general law, unpleasant odours are also unwholesome. Poor
nose! Its rights are little recognised. Our streets are filled with
nauseous odours and the personal uncleanliness of many
persons is an outrage to the sense of smell.

Sight has a right to beauty, symmetry, and elegance of form,
harmony of colours, grace of movement, and every pleasing
quality; to fine scenery, noble architecture, elegant furniture
and decorations, to exquisite works of art, and to all possible
beauty of person, costume, and adornment. Its rights are
denied by deprivation of these enjoyments, and it is outraged
by every obtrusion of ugliness.

Hearing has the right to sweet and melodious sounds, and
the grand harmonies of musical art: it is offended by noise,
confusion, and all harsh, dissonant and repulsive sounds.

There is scarcely a greater fault of manners, or offence
against the rights of others, than the unnecessary obtrusion
of painful, repulsive, or disgusting ideas or things. He
who conceals a pain, an affliction, or a misfortune, from
politeness, which is but another name for kindness or
benevolence, is a true hero.

With some people the chief staple of conversation consists
of the aches, illnesses, and misfortunes of themselves and their

neighbours; but such things ought never to be brought into a circle of refined society. We should no more pain or disgust others than inflict bodily injuries.

Thus we see that a book of behaviour may be a work of science and philosophy; that etiquette is based on principles and laws; that behaviour may have its foundation in mathematics; that grace of deportment is a noble art; that from the slightest act of complaisance to the highest moral duty the same great principles should govern us.

It has been said that each individual has the right to secure his own happiness in his own way, so long as he does not interfere with the equal right of every other. This is true, but not the whole truth. Each individual does secure the greatest possible happiness to himself when he promotes, in the highest degree, the happiness of all other beings. The good of one is the good of all; and were there no question of the feelings or opinions of others, every man would like to have his own respect and good opinion, which he could not do if he allowed himself to behave improperly in his own society. It is for this reason that, when a man behaves very badly, he is thought to be beside himself, or rather aside from himself, and quite oblivious of his own personality, which is a phenomenon of intoxication, as of other insanity; in which persons do the most unseemly and outrageous things, because they are unconscious of any recognition.

I believe that in the heart of a desert, or on an uninhabited island, a true gentleman would preserve all his dignity, and all his propriety and purity of conduct. I am sure that a true lady, in the privacy of her own apartment, is just as much a lady, as sweet, and delicate, and refined, and every way beautiful, as in the parlour, where I met her for a morning chat; or in the drawing room, where she is the cynosure of the evening party. Because everywhere the free being acts out his true nature. His life is instinctive and genuine, and his training has perfected his capabilities; so that habit is a second nature, which he does not violate.

Care of the Person

There can be no health, no comfort, no happiness in one's self; nor is it possible to be agreeable, or even tolerable to others, without attending to the common decencies of life in the care of our own bodies.

No one wishes to inspire others with disgust. No one ought to be willing, from laziness, inattention, or moroseness, to produce an unpleasant impression on any of the senses of those about him. No man can afford to cut himself off from human sympathy, which is an element of life.

The care of the person is the beginning of good manners. We enter here upon delicate ground; but the reader will see its necessity, and excuse our plainness of speech. The first moral and physical duty of every human being is to be clean. Cleanliness is akin to godliness. Filth is a violation of the rights of several of the senses. We see it; we feel it; sometimes we may be cheated into tasting it; and we smell it terribly. In all ways, and under all conditions, it is vile and bad, ill-mannered and immoral.

First of all, then, and above all, and as the prime condition of all excellence of character and beauty of life, be thoroughly and perfectly clean! The human organism is so constituted that no person can be absolutely clean without washing the whole surface of the body every day. Millions of pores are constantly exuding waste matter from the body. This matter, if allowed to remain, is filth; in any considerable quantity it is poison. Retained in the system, it is matter of disease.

It is not enough to change the undergarments often. Much is carried away, but much also adheres. In certain parts of the body, as under the arms and on the feet, it collects rapidly, and in a few hours has an offensive odour.

Cleanly persons have acute senses. I know ladies who can tell whether a person bathes daily the moment he comes into the room. Many a well-dressed man scents a parlour, as soon as he enters it, with the odour of his unwashed feet and gathered perspiration. We smell it everywhere – at theatres and churches, in steamboat cabins and omnibuses; everywhere we meet this mortifying and disgusting fact of personal uncleanliness. People whose senses are blunted by custom are unconscious of their personal conditions, but they are always liable to meet those to whom their lack of the first decency of life is a violent breach of good manners.

It is not difficult to take a daily bath – that is, to wash one's self all over thoroughly every morning. If face and hands feel better for it, why not the whole body? Cold water is better than warm; more invigorating, with less liability to chill. Washing the whole skin daily in cold water keeps that great purifying organ, with its myriads of glands and pores, in a pure, active, and healthy condition, and promotes the healthy action of every organ of the body. Dirt, on the other hand – the condensed perspiration, the solidified waste matter of the system – stops up the pores, and is a mechanical cause of disease, as well as an active poison. It is well to take a thorough washing every few days with hot water and soap, or ammonia, and this may be most conveniently done at night before going to bed; but the daily bath, for cleanliness and health, should be taken on rising in the morning.

If one has but a pint of water, he can wash the whole body with his hands, if he can do no better. If one has but two towels, one can be dipped in the water and used to wash with, and the other to wipe. If there is a shallow tub to stand in, the towel can be used with as much water as it will hold.

Some prefer a sponge, but one may do very well with a towel. Begin with face, head, and arms. At least the scalp and roots of the hair should have the benefit of the daily bath. Then dip the towel afresh and wash down the front of the body and legs; double lengthwise, dip, and, beginning at the neck, wash down the back; finish by carefully washing the feet. Now a thorough wiping and brisk rubbing of the whole body; and finish, if you can, with flesh brush, crash, or Turkish towel.

Washing the head promotes the growth and beauty of the hair, and prevents headache. Washing the teeth and gums with a hard brush and cold water keeps the teeth white and clear of tartar, the gums red and firm, and the breath sweet. Washing the whole skin keeps it clean and sweeter, often, than all perfumes; prevents colds, coughs, chilliness, rheumatism, and gives the complexion a pure, clear, fresh tint of health, better than all cosmetics. Cleanliness of the whole person is the first element of refinement.

Every sleeping or dressing room should be furnished with plenty of water, pure and good soap, plenty of soft and hard towels, a broad, shallow tub to stand in, combs, nail brushes, tooth brushes, hair brushes, flesh brushes. Of these strictly personal things everyone should have his own – not to be used by another except under pressure of the direst necessity.

To breathe pure air by night and by day is one of the most important of the conditions of health. Every room should have thorough ventilation. A window, open at the top ever so little, allows the foul, breathed air to pass off, and fresh air to enter. Where several persons are in a room, railway compartment, or carriage, each one deprives the air of oxygen, and loads it with carbonic acid, and the waste matter of his body, which no one should be required to breathe. Fresh air is an element of health, manners, and morals. To live without it is a slow suicide; to deprive others of it approximates to homicide.

These may seem small matters, but small matters make up the sum of life. And some of these are matters of great importance. When an unwashed person comes into a room, he fills it in a few minutes with the effluvia of his body. Five or six such persons make the atmosphere disgusting to the senses, and poisonous to the constitution. Our churches, concert-rooms, theatres, all places filled by people of ordinary habits of life become pestiferous, unless great attention is paid to their ventilation. Soldiers in camps, and prisoners in jails, have often bred pestilence, and there is no doubt that many lives are shortened by the bad air of our fashionable assemblies.

Cleanliness of clothing should correspond with cleanliness of the person. It is, in fact, part of the same thing. The entire under-clothing should be changed often. Bed clothing should be thoroughly aired every day, and often changed. The bed clothes in the morning are filled with the emanations of the body during several hours. In no case must it be re-absorbed. We must sleep in no garment that we have worn during the day, and wear by day none that we have worn at night. When we take off our clothes every article to be worn again should be well shaken, and hung where it can be aired during the night. So the bed should be spread open in the morning, and sheets and blankets well shaken and aired. These are conditions alike of decency and health. Persons, garments, breath, should be kept pure and sweet, so as to offend no sense of our own or another's. The nails should be nicely cut, and kept perfectly clean – this is a mark of the most careful breeding; so of the bright cleanliness of hair and teeth.

For health, beauty, sweetness, and use, the teeth should be kept clean from the earliest period, by daily and careful washing. No speck of tartar should be allowed to gather on them, no food to lodge between them; but they should be ever bright and clean. Foul and rotten teeth are disgusting to the sight, and still more to the smell. Keep them thoroughly clean; wash teeth and mouth with antiseptics if the teeth show the least taint, and at the first sign of decay, consult a good dentist.

The natural functions of the body should be performed with regularity. The diet should be of a character to produce a full daily evacuation of the bowels. This is a necessity of decency and health. It is seldom needful to take medicine. We have but to eat healthy food to keep entirely free from constipation, and all its attendant and often distressing maladies. Good brown bread, made of unbolted wheat meal, porridge of coarsely ground wheat or oatmeal (the former is best); fruit, as apples, pears, berries, stewed prunes, figs; spinach, and other greens and vegetables, keep the bowels in a healthy condition. Injections of cold water are better than any aperients or cathartics. Health is a condition of beauty, activity, and enjoyment. Certain states of illness unfit a person for society. We should never intrude upon others any object of disgust, least of all ourselves. A man with a swollen face, or sore eyes, an eruption, a severe cold, a catarrh, or in a condition which in any way offends the sight, smell, or hearing, must refrain from general society. It is our duty to give pleasure – we have no right to inflict pain.

All right care of the person must have its basis in health, which is the condition of beauty, grace, happiness in ourselves, and the power of conferring happiness on others. Health gives brightness to the eye, the rosy flush to the complexion, the silken gloss of the hair, the charm of animated expression to the features, and all the grace and charm of an abounding vitality – a fullness of life.

To be healthy – to possess this first condition of the enjoyment of life, the spring of good behaviour – we must observe the conditions of health, and avoid the causes of disease. We must be clean and pure in our persons, our habits and our morals. We must bathe in pure water, breathe pure air, and live on pure food, and shun every cause of nervous abuse and exhaustion. We must expand and develop body and mind by exercise, avoid sensuality and sloth, be temperate and chaste, and beware of every kind of vicious indulgence.

In food, we should seek that which will give us the best nourishment, in the purest and most agreeable forms. The type of the most natural, and therefore best and most healthful food is fruit and the seeds of plants. Children, and all persons of simple, natural tastes, love apples, peaches, grapes, strawberries, etc. Then comes bread in all its varieties, then milk and its products, and eggs. In the choice of food we should follow our tastes and instincts. What food would a lover like best to see his mistress eat? Not bacon or sausages. Not anything that would taint her breath, or destroy the delicacy of her complexion. The more simple the food, and the less it is composed of the bodies of dead animals, the better for health and purity of life.

All stimulants – all intoxicants – all narcotics are dangerous. They always injure, they often destroy. Tea, coffee, tobacco, opium, narcotics which 'cheer but not inebriate', are really intoxicants, though they act differently from beer, wine, and spirits. They excite the nerves, and therefore weaken them. I earnestly advise the young to let them all alone; and I advise parents to save their children from acquiring the habit of using any kind of stimulants, however innocent many may esteem them. They are all useless for nourishment; all dangerous to the nervous systems of those who use them.

Tobacco, the worst of narcotics, because the most widely used, is fortunately almost entirely restricted to one sex. The good taste of women has so far protected them from its pollution. And there are few men who, even if they smoke themselves, would be willing to see their mothers, wives, sisters, sweethearts, or daughters filling their drawing rooms or the streets with tobacco smoke. But if tobacco be right and good for men, why should women be debarred from its use and enjoyment. If the boy of twelve may smoke, why not his sister? If the lord, why not the lady; if the earl, why not the countess; if the prince, why not the princess? But the use of tobacco produces in many persons disgust and nausea, simply by its presence. It taints the breath, the hair, and beard, and the clothing. Can it be good manners to use anywhere what is prohibited in all polite assemblies, and wherever women congregate? Can it be nice to do what banishes people to rooms specially provided for the purpose, and makes them objects of disgust to many men, and a great majority of women?

There can be no doubt that the use of tobacco is a cause of many deadly, nervous diseases. No one can point to a single benefit the world has derived from it during the three centuries since it came into use. It could be entirely abandoned, not only without loss, but with great advantage to human health and well-being.

In our day, gentlemen are never seen intoxicated – ladies, who deserved the name, never were. Women left the table before men began to drink. Drunkenness is out of fashion for either sex, and it may be hoped that this fashion of moderation, if not of abstinence, will spread like fashions in dress, from the higher to the lower classes. Certainly, no one who wishes to preserve health or character will ever risk the excessive use of intoxicating liquors, and the only safe course for great numbers is to abstain from them altogether.

CLOTHES

Man alone, of all creatures, needs to be concerned about clothes. Nature has provided in the most fitting and beautiful manner for all beasts, birds, fishes, and insects. Look at the glossy hair, mane, and tail of the horse, the markings of the tiger and leopard, the soft fur of cat or beaver, the brilliant, graceful, and wonderfully painted plumage of the birds, the fishes' shining scales, and all the marvels of the insect world. For warmth and protection from rain and heat, and for ornament, we imitate and appropriate the natural costumes of the animal and vegetable world. We wear skins, fur, wool, feathers, and the fibrous coats and seed coverings of plants. We ornament ourselves with metals, minerals, crystals, coral, pearls, feathers, leaves, and flowers. The three kingdoms of nature furnishes us with all the colours of the rainbow. Fishes give purple, insects cochineal, and even the coal that warms us, yields up to chemistry the most gorgeous tints for our adornment.

In an Eden clime and shameless innocence, with perfect health and freedom from all deformities, clothing might not be needed. There are tropical regions where people go almost, and children entirely naked, and many persons believe that this exposure of the whole surface of the body to the action of air and light has great advantages. Certainly, the portions of our skin habitually exposed are the most healthy. Even in this climate of England, our ancestors wore very little clothing. Highland regiments are contented with their kilts, and the North American Indian, where the winters are far more severe, went nearly naked in the coldest weather – being, as he said, 'all face'.

To us, however, clothing has become necessary for warmth and decency, for the concealment of bodily defects, for custom, fashion, grace, and elegance. We should seek, therefore, to clothe ourselves in the best manner for all our needs – to dress for comfort, convenience, use, and beauty; for our own good and pleasure, and for the comfort and delight of all around us.

The entire costume should be neat, clean, appropriate, modest, unobtrusive; not expressive of ostentation, vanity, or self-conceit; suitable to our condition and fortune; becoming, elegant, and such as to produce a good impression upon all who see us. Dress is a language speaking to the eye – and we should not use bad language. Dress is an indication of character, and a means of influence, and of education. Shabbiness of dress is a demoralisation. Behaviour is influenced by costume. People who are careless in their dress are likely to be careless in their habits and manners; when they put on nice clothes they assume a corresponding behaviour.

There may be times and circumstances when people do well to put on sackcloth and ashes, and dress for humiliation and mortification. In the sadness of a great calamity we put off gay attire; and though we may not obtrude our grief by mourning weeds, we should not wear bright colours. But in our ordinary life and its enjoyments, we ought to be in harmony with the beauty of the world around us – with earth and skies, trees and flowers; and to be as well clothed, at least, as birds and beasts.

There is some style of dress more suited than any others to every per son and every condition. The labourer, the domestic servant, the artisan, the tradesman, the professional man, each looks best in his own befitting costume. It is pleasant, travelling over the continent, to see the neat becoming dress of every rank and condition; no one ever aping the other; each one preserving his own characterand dignity, respecting himself and respected by others.

For cleanliness and protection from cold, everyone should wear under-shirts and drawers, which may be of cotton, linen, wool, or silk. Cotton is warmer than linen, less irritating to sensitive nerves than any but the finest wool; while the latter and spun silk are better non-conductors of heat. It is a matter of individual taste and comfort. Some ladies wear complete, close-fitting hosiery undergarments, covering the whole body, and over them the chemise and drawers, the latter of cotton or linen in summer, and flannel in winter.

And they do well who also wear good woollen or worsted stockings nine months in twelve in England, even if they have fine thread or silk ones over them.

Multitudes of people in England, and not alone those of the poorer class, and especially women, suffer from throat and lung diseases and rheumatism for lack of good warm underclothing. In such cases a thick undershirt, and flannel drawers and petticoats are far better than all the drugs of the dispensaries; and doctors would do well to examine all poor patients, and some not poor, but who have the habit of dressing poorly in this respect, and make their prescription accordingly. Cleanliness, coal, and flannel, are for great numbers the most needed medicines.

A good warm nightgown is a necessity. No one should ever sleep at night in any garment worn by day. And all clothing, night and day, should bewell shaken and aired, and kept perfectly clean and sweet. There is a colliery in Belgium where the clothes of the miners are washed daily. Every miner on coming from the pit takes a bath, and his garments go to the laundry, and are ready for him to put on fresh and clean next morning.

Every man should have plenty of good, well-fitting, nicely made shirts. In these days of cheap fabrics and sewing machines there is no excuse for not having good ones and a good supply. I confess to a great repugnance to any sort of shams in this direction; detached collars seem a necessity of fashion, but not false wristbands and false fronts. The shirt should be changed often enough not to need them. It is rather extravagant to wear two shirts a day, but a gentleman who goes much into society can scarcely wear less than six a week. No exact rule can be given but this – no one should ever wear any garment, seen or unseen, which would show that it had been worn to sight or smell. Any article that offends either sense belongs to the washerwoman.

The London costermongers, male and female, are well shod. It is a redeeming trait in their characters. Landing on the French coast, the first thing you observe is the strong, clean, proper costumes of the peasant women, with their white caps, coarse woollen gowns, good stockings, and strong leather or wooden shoes. One can hardly be too careful about the make and fit of boots and shoes, in avoiding corns, bunions, and slovenliness. Cheapness is no economy.

Live on sixpence a day, – but wear good leather; and never wear a too tight, or an ill-fitting, or an ugly formed shoe. To a certain degree one may – perhaps I should say must – conform to the fashion, however absurd it may be; but I doubt the necessity of wearing a boot with a heel two inches high placed under the hollow of the foot. Fashion may adorn, but should never outrage, nature.

Men wear hats in considerable variety, and one may choose, or let a friend choose for him the style that suits him best, high or low crown, broad brim, or narrow; but the hat, whatever its form, should be light, and the fit perfect. Be sure that it is large enough; because it is easy to pad a little under the lining. Be sure that it is light and easy, for I have no doubt that many brains are injured by oppressive head gear. It is well to have a soft light hat or cap for common use, and for travelling, and keep the well- brushed stove-pipe affair for more solemn occasions.

The cut of the hair, and the style of the beard may generally be left to the hairdresser. If you cannot trust to his taste in the matter, use your own, or consult someone who has an interest in your good appearance. But it is my solemn opinion that razors may be entirely banished from the earth with great advantage to health and manliness. I see no good reason why any man should shave. It is a fashion, like that of judges and barristers, and the speaker and clerks of the House of Commons wearing absurd white wigs of curled horse hair. The bishops left them off but lately; and why the others stick to such tomfoolery passes comprehension. A becoming and distinctive costume – yes: but these wigs are not becoming. Never let hair or beard show that you have used oil or pomatum. If hair or skin require any artificial aid, the art must never be apparent. I do not say that no lady may use white powder for a sallow skin, or a tinge of rouge upon a pallid cheek or lip; or darken the hair, or brows, or lashes; but I do say that no such device should ever betray itself by careless or extravagant use. Have I not seen women who looked as if they had laid their faces into the bread trough, and so rouged that one could see it across the street?

The fashions of dressing women's hair have for some years been artificial, extravagant, and outrageous – unnatural to such a degree that all women who care for real grace and beauty should revolt against them. Now that 'the rage' has passed away, we can see how hideous were the chignons of a few years ago, stuck like a pumpkin on the back of the head – worn even by ladies on horseback in Rotten Row – the hideous monstrosities bobbing up and down behind the stove-pipe hats. I do not see that the modifications of wildly stuffed manes that succeeded them were more becoming, or that the towers carried the hats or bonnets ten inches into the air were better. A fine head of natural hair is a glory to a woman – but is a mass of false hair, or jute, or padding any particular glory.

'False hair' is an unpleasant phrase; for we want nothing false in, or out, or about us. But I see no more harm in wearing the hair of other people, than the fur or feathers of other animals. It is the monstrosities of form and size that I object to. A woman's long, glossy hair, is one of the loveliest of nature's adornments, and may be worn in many fashions of exquisite beauty.

Dyeing the hair is doubtful. Some dyes have an unpleasant smell – some are poisonous. It seems to me better that a woman should wear her grey or white hair than to colour it; and to change the natural colour of young hair to some fashionable tint is a great folly. All natural colours suit the complexion – and grey or white hair looks better upon a worn and faded face than artificial black or brown.

Fashion is inexplicable. No one can tell whence it comes, or by what laws it is governed; but it rules a large part of the world. In Asia and Northern Africa dress has little changed for centuries. On many parts of the continent, the common people have kept to their costumes for a long period; but the higher classes of Europe and America have for some centuries varied their forms and styles of dress, as if some potentate more powerful than any monarch had given the law, and all hastened to obey it. Look through the fashion plates of the last hundred years, and you will see how the ugliest things ever worn by man or woman have been the fashion in different periods. There is certainly some style of dress more fitting, and more beautiful for every style of person, than any other – but fashion compels all to dress alike, and all to dress in the most absurd and unbecoming manner. Bonnets are at one time like coal scuttles; at another a mere wisp of ribbon and flowers. Waists are close under the arms or down to the hips. Skirts cling to the legs, or expand to huge balloons. They come but half way down the calf, or drag a yard upon the ground. What is esteemed beautiful in one year becomes frightful the next. We all see the absurdity of fashion; yet we are all obliged to more or less conform to it – and I think the conformity should be rather less. A good rule is to always keep inside the fashion, but to dress so as not to be very noticeably different from others, with the difference a sensible and tasteful one. When fashion requires a woman to uncover her shoulders and bosom, a modest woman will keep on the side of modesty, and a tasteful woman on the side of taste.

And health ought always to be considered. A woman bares her arms and shoulders with the chance of bronchitis; she changes woollen stockings for thread and silk at the risk of rheumatism; she laces herself into the fashionable wasp or hourglass waist in deadly peril from compressed lungs, heart, liver, and stomach – spinal disease – impeded respiration – impeded circulation. It is true that a certain vigour of constitution may triumph over all the usual causes of disease, but it is also true that they are death to thousands.

The clothing of both sexes should be good, substantial, becoming in style and colour, adapted to size and figure, made of genuine, lasting materials, and so made and worn as to best answer every purpose of dress. To get good articles, and have them well and nicely made is the best economy. Good firm cloth, and textures of every kind, are cheaper in the end than shoddy and shams. A good article will wear, turn, change, make over, and do for others when you can make it do no longer. Double the price and you get treble or quadruple the wear; and have the benefit of a rich, elegant, and beautiful article. A really good coat, hat, pair of boots, or dress, looks better after a year's service than a sham, cheap, new one. The same rule applies to every article of use or ornament. Avoid imitations, and all false trimmings and jewellery. Rather go without anything that can be spared than wear what you are or ought to be ashamed of. This is not only good taste, but good economy. A pair of gloves at four shillings will outwear three pairs at two shillings, and look better to the last moment. Find a good hatter, boot maker, tailor; have everything made to measure, and everything as good as you can buy – sure that the best at a reasonable price will be the cheapest – for it costs as much to make most articles of poor materials as of good. This rule applies to most articles of ladies' dress as well as gentlemen's; but if a dress is to be worn but once or twice, the cheaper the stuff, and the less the labour expended upon it, the better.

Englishmen wear grey, brown, purple plaids and stripes in the morning; in the afternoon, black, or dark-blue frock coats, and for dinner and evening dress the black swallow tail coat, black cloth waistcoat with open bosom, and black cloth trousers. It is useless to quarrel with these fashions. We have only to conform to them. Only, when Englishmen travel on the Continent, they would do well to conform a little to continental tastes and habits; and not visit churches, or go to theatres in rough grey 'tourists' suits' and 'wide awakes'.

Rather dark gloves are worn in the morning; lavender or buff in the afternoon; and with full evening dress, pure white; though some of the lighter tints may be admissible. Ladies try to match the colours of dress, boots, and gloves. At least, they choose harmonious tints; colours that suit their hair and complexions, and that also suit each other. Englishwomen are said to be faulty in these matters, while Frenchwomen are almost invariably perfect; and it is quite true that one can generally distinguish Englishwomen in Paris by the style of dress, the colours they wear, and their manner of wearing them. The English style is wanting in elegance, grace, propriety, and harmony. The colours are stronger, and fighting with each other, and the effect is what people call 'glaring' and 'dowdy'. No doubt there are English ladies who dress with exquisite taste and delicacy, and who, therefore, cannot be distinguished from the most refined ladies of Paris.

Dress is the outward and visible sign of inward and spiritual grace, or of the want of it. It is an indication of character – of order, neatness, taste, elegance, modesty, simplicity, pride, vanity, ostentation, and many other good or bad qualities, when people freely select their costumes. But fashion does much to bring people into uniformity of habits and lives, and to destroy naturalness and the picturesque interest of society. All dress should display and adorn the beauty of the human form, and conceal its defects, but never distort and deform.

Be careful in uniting colours to complexion and hair, and also to each other. A rose, red, pales a rosy complexion; a delicate green heightens it. Yellow makes a dark skin look violet. Violet makes people look yellow, and turns blue to green. Blue suits well to blondes; while orange makes fair complexions blue, and turns yellow to green. Lustreless white raises the tone of all colours, and is unsuited therefore, to any disagreeable tint. Black lowers the tone of all colours, and whitens the skin, while it deepens the flush of the cheeks. Yellow, lilac, and red are the most trying colours; and pale tints of blue, rose, violet, and neutral tints, pearls, greys, and soft warm browns, the most generally becoming.

The cost of dress must be a matter of conscience. Superfluities and luxuries of attire can hardly be admitted when people around us are shivering with cold, and have scarcely enough rags to cover their nakedness. It is said that a lady can dress as a lady for fifteen pounds a year. An ordinary allowance is twenty pounds; but there are many who spend on dress enough to comfortably maintain several families. A gentleman can dress very well on ten pounds a year; but one can also easily spend that sum on gloves and bouquets for his button-hole. Money is better spent on dress than on many other luxuries; better than on costly food, which is a waste of not only money, but health and life; better than on costly wines or tobacco; better than on any bad habits and vices. It is even a moral duty to dress well, tastefully, becomingly, and so as to give pleasure to those about us; but the cost of dress must be limited by our duties to others. We cannot eat luxuries while others starve; we cannot be clothed in purple and fine linen while Lazarus lies naked at the gate.

A good rule in dress as in manners is to observe and imitate those who have the best taste and breeding, with such variation as circumstances and conditions require. Every man should adapt his costume to his condition and pursuits in life. There is one style of dress suitable to a clergyman, another to a physician, another to a tradesman; and artisans or labourers must have clothing suited to their employments when at work, and to their position in life at all times. To dress beyond our means, and a manner unsuited to one's position, is to dress like a 'snob'. There is a costume or style of dress most becoming for persons of every position in life, and to that they should carefully conform; since they are certain to be most respected in so doing. The maid is not to imitate her mistress, but to dress neatly, tastefully, and becomingly in the style suited to her calling.

We dress for our own health, comfort, and sense of beauty and fitness, first; and then to please, attract, satisfy, and delight all around us. We have no right to offend by rags or filth; nor even by uncouth forms and unpleasant colours. To dress decently and neatly is a duty – to dress so as to increase the happiness of others should be our delight.

Deportment

Deportment is the manner of carrying one's self; carriage, manner, or behaviour. Good looks are very desirable; but far more depends upon behaviour. The neatness of the person, upon which we have so strongly insisted, is a part of behaviour; so is dress, which is a mode of expression; and which gives us methods of enhancing and displaying beauties, as well as of concealing defects.

But a handsome and well-dressed person may be awkward and constrained in manner, stiff or slouching in gait; angular and extravagant in gesture; sullen, haughty, insolent, cold, rude; or shy and sheepish; or craving, fawning, and impertinently familiar. There are a hundred graces and excellencies of manner in the position of the body, the attitudes, movements, gestures, poses of the head, carriage of the arms, placing of the feet, and all those nameless proprieties and charms, which are in some the unconscious and spontaneous expression of their natures, and in others, are more or less acquired by the faculty of imitation, and careful training and culture.

It needs no argument to prove that beauty was not intended alone nor chiefly to give happiness to its possessors; and that, consequently, society has pre-eminent rights in regard to it. The possession of beauty, then, brings with it a heavy responsibility. You have no right to conceal, mar, or spoil it. You have no right to lose it, by neglect of health, or any habit which tends to the destruction of beauty. You have no right to hide it in ugly and deforming costumes. You have no right to mar it by any lack of grace and propriety of manners.

Attitude, the simple pose of the body, is a matter of great importance. It reveals character and breeding. A gentleman or lady stands confessed. Awkwardness and vulgarity are shown in attitude. Once at a theatre, I saw a house, full from pit to gallery, give three rounds of plaudits at the simple silent act of a peasant girl sitting down in a chair. It was nothing else. It had nothing to do with the plot of the piece. It was simply and only sitting down. But what grace, and beauty, and exquisite delicacy were revealed in every movement, and the quiet, easy attitude into which she sank, was a living picture that charmed every beholder.

The first polite accomplishment is to know how to stand. An awkward person is in a perpetual fidget, and changes incessantly from one uneasy posture to another. He knows not where to put his feet, and his hands are utterly superfluous. There they go – now behind him, now into his pockets – now under his coat tails; and so he fidgets and shifts his weight from one leg to the other, and becomes all the more awkward from the consciousness of his awkwardness. If he could possibly forget himself, and let his limbs take care of themselves, it would be better.

The conditions of good deportment are simplicity, or absence of affectation; ease, or absence of constraint, fussiness or fidgetiness; and self-possession, self-command, or freedom from timidity. The whole is comprehended in simplicity. Simple manners are good manners. Quiet, easy, calm self-possession gives unconscious grace and dignity.

The perfection of good manners is repose; not languor, nor affected coolness, nor hauteur, but the calm, quiet, simple dignity of the true gentleman or lady. Such persons stand easily on both legs, but bearing a little more weight on one than the other; the toes turn out easily, the head is a little turned, the body is never kept a hard straight line,– but all is natural ease, and unaffected grace. The arms hang naturally from the shoulders, the hands are in some quiet easy position, the fingers curve gracefully, with slight partings between the first and second, and the third and fourth. There is no stiffness, no uneasy shifting and fidgeting, no moving of fingers or features, but all is easy, rounded and graceful as a statue. It is worth some pains to be a man of good standing in society.

One should learn no less to sit at ease. Formerly ladies were trained to sit upright, and never touch the back of a chair. They might as well have sat on stools. It is now permitted to lean, and, where one is intimate, to lounge; but it is never permitted to be awkward or ungraceful – never to stretch out the legs, or spread them apart. No gentleman tilts up his chair or sits astride it; or fusses with his feet, or drums with his fingers. He sits like a gentleman – it is difficult to describe how; but everyone recognises it, and everyone should do his best to imitate it; or by being a gentleman, to make it the natural expression of his character.

The gait and air in movement are more complex matters. To walk well, easily, gracefully, is a very important accomplishment. What we do so often we should do well; and walking is not only useful and necessary, but a great enjoyment; and every man's gait is the expression of his natural and acquired character. The gait may be heavy or light; neat or clumsy; erect or slouching, or 'slobbery', quick or slow; awkward or graceful. The walk or carriage of the body expresses every virtue and every vice, every beauty and every deformity; habits and diseases. As the mind and heart are expressed in bodily movements – these movements in return act upon the intellectual and moral faculties. The raw recruit drilled into the accomplished soldier, has his mind 'set up', and brought into soldierly habits, as well as his body. The training of the body certainly affects the mind, and there is more than an analogy between physical and moral uprightness and grace, and the drill sergeant and dancing master exercise a deeper influence than has commonly been recognised.

The drill sergeant takes a booby, a clodhopper, a graceless vagabond. He straightens him up, turns out his toes, brings back his shoulders, throws out his chest, and in a few months makes a soldier of him – a straight, well set, firm, alert, active man – a self-reliant, courageous soldier. And he is a different man forever after. His character has changed with his bearing. Much of the ignoble and awkward in his nature, which found habitual expression in his mien, has been suppressed, driven back, or rooted out like weeds; while the finer and more manly characteristics are brought into activity, strengthened by exercise, and rendered habitual; and this man, to the last day of his life, shows something of the manner and bearing, and exhibits correspondingly the character of a soldier.

And the dancing master, or teacher of gymnastics and the graces of posture and movement, performs a similar but more refined office. It is his business to bring out, develop, cultivate, and render habitual, the dignities and graces of polished life. He teaches the pupil how he should carry his head, strengthen his limbs, stand, sit, bow, walk, or dance, if dancing is the fashion of the time. He trains him into the external expression of a pure and refined, and elegant character; and, as in the case of the soldier, the external acts upon the internal, and a man becomes really what he endeavours to appear. And in this we have much of the philosophy of education and social culture. By exercise our dormant faculties are brought into action. Internal action may be induced by the external expression. Be what you would appear, certainly; but also appear what you wish to be. Assume the air and manner of calmness, and it will help you to be calm. Put on the natural action of any faculty, and it will excite its activity. Thus we may refine and purify the character. To 'assume a virtue if you have it not', is hypocrisy, only when it is done for some unworthy object. But when we are trying to reform our lives and make ourselves the best we can be, we may begin with the external deportment.

The carriage of the body, and habits of dexterity, grace, and elegance are of great importance. Children, it is said, are always graceful – they are simple, unconscious, unrestrained, unaffected; and the attitudes and movements of a child ought to be as pretty as those of a kitten or a bird. But we fall into bad habits; stoop until we grow round-shouldered; get into awkward, lounging ways; carry our hands uneasily as if they did not belong to us, and make ourselves generally disagreeable. A little care; a little resolute training; the observation and imitation of ease and grace in others will do much to remedy their besetting sins. If a boy or man will every day stand with his back against a wall, and carry himself with physical uprightness, he will soon cure himself of a drooping spine. If he will resolutely let his arms hang quietly at his side, he will conquer the bashful tendency to fidget with his fingers. If a man will daily open his chest, and breathe full breaths for some minutes, he will improve his health and figure. Every schoolmaster and schoolmistress ought to be somewhat of a drill-sergeant, and attend to the personal appearance and habits, carriage and manners of the pupils. This is the speciality of the dancing master and gymnast, no doubt – but as every school cannot have its special teacher of gymnastics and dancing, all our teachers should be capable of giving the rudiments at least of refined carriage and manners.

In the absence of direct teaching, much is done by unconscious or conscious imitation – only we should know what models we ought to admire. Copies of the great Vance are to be met in all the London streets and music halls. The worst habits of more exalted personages have found multitudes of imitators. Everyone who, by position or talents, grace or beauty, makes an impression upon others, is a teacher of manners. How little do people think of their responsibilities!

To walk easily the body must be erect, but not stiff; the arms must swing, not too far; the chest expanded for full breathing; the shoulders held back; the toes a little, but not too much, turned out; and all the muscles of the foot brought into a springy, elastic action. A fine gait in man or woman, as in many animals, is one of the prettiest things in the world. Avoid walking stiffly, slovenly, dumpily; and ladies, because they wear long dresses, must not therefore be careless of their feet, turning in their toes, or lifting their skirts with their heels.

Walking is good exercise; but one may have too much of it. It is a relief from sedentary and monotonous employment; but where there is much brain work, long walks are too exhausting. A short, brisk walk, quickening the circulation, and consequently the breathing, is better. Delicate persons and invalids are injured by long walks. The vital forces are limited, and must be used with economy.

In our efforts to live a good life, satisfactory to ourselves and pleasing to our fellow-creatures, there are many things we must carefully avoid. We must avoid every action that is painful, disgusting, offensive, or troublesome to those about us. We must 'cease to do evil', and then 'learn to do well', in the little things of life as well as m the most important. We talk of rights and freedom, but no one has a right to do the smallest wrong to himself or another. There is no freedom but the right to do right. Every improper act really injures both ourselves and many others. We have no right in any way to diminish our power of being good and doing good. A musician, playing out of tune, hurts his own ear, and offends the ears of all who hear him. The man who does a distasteful act when quite alone hurts his own sense of propriety; if he does it with others he offends them and injures himself.

No one has the right to appear in public in a dirty, disorderly, or unbecoming costume. In this matter there is a world of difference between London and Paris. You may go every day to the most frequented public resorts in Paris without ever seeing a man, much less a woman, in offensive attire. Can the same be said of any place of public resort in London?

What belongs to the toilet should never be done in public. One may repair an accident, put up a stray ringlet, arrange a shawl, tie a string; but one may not comb the hair, clean the nails, or touch the nose or ears. It is not delicate to scratch one's self. Only under the most urgent necessity can one blow his nose in company. It may be wiped, not blown, if it can be avoided, especially at table. In England no one is ever seen to spit – I wish the same could be said of the rest of Europe and America. Where spitting is. unavoidable, use a pocket handkerchief; and in all such matters take great care never to be for one instant an object of disgust. In this matter the French and Germans are nearly as bad as the Americans; and Vienna is the only place I know of where the churches are furnished with spit-boxes. It is not very long since the English were as bad as their neighbours; and every reform makes us more hopeful about others.

The use of tobacco in any form is a nuisance that no society ought to tolerate. It makes the breath, the hair, the clothes disgusting. Men who smoke are put in separate rooms in houses and clubs, and in separate compartments on railways. No gentleman ever presumes to smoke in the presence of a lady. Such, at least, were English manners not many years ago; but they have been Germanised of late, and thereby less civilised. A prince smoking in the presence of a lady is a very unpleasant spectacle; and the ladies of England would do well to set their faces resolutely against such an un-English proceeding.

A gentleman must not have the taint of spirits upon his breath, nor ever be seen with the slightest sign of intoxication. Drinking is a low vice, and gets lower and lower as the people rise above it. Total abstinence from all intoxicants is the only safety for many, and may be a good rule for most; but there can be no doubt that temperance, and the careful avoidance of the least excess, is the rule for all. In these days no gentleman is ever seen flushed with wine, thick of speech, unsteady of gait, and with his brain excited or stupefied with drink. I wish it could be said that no lady ever was or is in such condition.

And I think those who wish to live purely and delicately, and never injure themselves or offend others, must avoid coarse eating as well as coarse drinking. There are kinds of food which are uncleanly and unsafe. I do not see how a lady or gentleman can eat bacon, or sausages, or pork in any form. Onions taint the breath too much for general society. If all eat onions it is different Cabbage is doubtful. Some kinds of fish, as herrings, not only taint the breath, but their odour exudes from the skin. A pure and inoffensive diet seems to me a cardinal point in good behaviour. Gross feeding, in quality and quantity, produces obstructions, obesity, heaviness of body and mind, and so many unpleasant diseases and conditions as to unfit people for society, and even for life; and gluttony is worse, if possible, than drunkenness, both being rightly reckoned among the deadly sins, any tendency to which every well-meaning person should carefully avoid.

Try to free yourself from all annoying habits. Do not make disagreeable noises, nor any noises that can be avoided, in eating or drinking. Never hum or whistle, unless quite alone. To do either in company may be very disagreeable. Beware of snuffling, or any unpleasant sound of nose, or mouth, or breathing. Sleep with your mouth closed, so as never to snore. So resolutely guard your life from any impropriety that you cannot even dream of one; for a careful conscience never sleeps. It is the strong desire and resolute will to be right and do right that is wanting in those who do wrong.

In a word, avoid everything wrong, everything improper, everything that hurts yourself or that may be annoying or disagreeable to others; and do what is just, right, good, and pleasant to all about you. The desire and will to do this is the foundation of good behaviour. There must be a good heart, then a good understanding, taste, tact, delicacy, all that belongs to an active benevolence, extending to the little things of life as well as the greater and more important. Often we cannot see our own faults; therefore, we should invite friendly criticism, never be hurt by it, and do our best to profit by it.

MANNERS

Men are gregarious – made to live in societies – their well-being and happiness very largely depending upon their associations with each other. We come together in friendship, love, mutual help, and in many ways to benefit or amuse one another. We live in families, neighbourhoods, societies, churches, and all sorts of industrial, benevolent, civil, and military organisations. We are parents, children, brothers, sisters, masters, servants, variously related to those around us – bound together by common interests, and we should all be working together for the general good; all for each, each for all. The welfare and happiness of society depends upon the behaviour of its members to each other – upon what we call manners – upon the way in which each one makes himself pleasant, agreeable, and useful to all around him.

I have already spoken of the care of the person necessary that we may avoid giving disgust or pain, and which will make our presence a delight; of dress for comfort, health, and a decent, and even elegant adornment; of the carriage of the body, or deportment; and now we must consider how people should treat each other so as to promote each other's happiness.

The foundation of good manners is in that love of our neighbour which religion requires as the second duty of every human being, and which naturally follows from fulfilling the first; for it is impossible for us to love God without loving also our fellow men. This love gives us the desire to promote their wellbeing and happiness. If we have this love for them we can never treat them with rudeness or injustice; but always with respect, sincerity, kindness, delicacy, and true charity. A good man has the foundation of good manners.

The Christian must be essentially, and in his feelings and intentions, a gentleman, though he may outwardly fall short of the courtesy taught by St Paul.

One of the first points of good breeding is to respect the person and rights of others – never to intrude upon them; never to be rude; never to be in any way troublesome or offensive. We have something to learn in this matter from our neighbours. When a Frenchman enters the company of others, if only in a wine shop or an omnibus, he deferently salutes the company by raising his hat, as much as to say 'by your good leaves, ladies and gentlemen.' He never enters a shop or café without politely saluting the person in charge, and he does the same on leaving. 'If you please', is on his lips continually, and at the slightest possible offence, or the least accidental encroachment, he gracefully begs your pardon. In the greatest crowd in Paris, one is never crowded. Each person is careful not to incommode his neighbour. No matter how many may assemble at the doors of a theatre or other place of amusement they never crowd each other; they never struggle for the best places; there is no ugly rush with women screaming from pain or fright, and possibly fainting and being trampled upon. In England, in several instances, persons have been trampled to death by crowds at the doors of theatres and other assemblages; and at the pit-entrance of the Haymarket Theatre, at a public execution, at the funeral of the Duke of Wellington, at the marriage of the Prince of Wales. Dozens or scores of people have been trampled to death, and there is always the risk of such a calamity so long as people do not respect the personal rights of each other. To press against any person is a violation of such rights. It is a trespass – an assault. You have no right to come into personal contact, nor even close proximity, to any man without his permission; and in a gentleman's conduct to a lady, this rule is more imperative.

Every one has also the right of privacy – the right to be alone – the right of silence and seclusion; and even in the intimacy of family life, this right should be carefully regarded. One should never approach another without some indication of welcome; never enter the private apartment of another without being sure that it is not an annoyance.

There is need of tact in these matters, and at the least sign of disquiet, we should increase our distance. We need not be shy or bashful, however pretty and graceful a certain amount of these qualities may be, but in fondness and in justice, as well as from self-respect, and the desire to stand well with others, we should carefully avoid intrusiveness.

It is for the elder person to first salute, invite, or welcome the younger; for the person in a higher social position to recognise or address one in a lower; for a lady to be the first to salute, speak, or hold out her hand to a gentleman. When two strangers meet, if there is any obvious difference in age, rank, or position, it should be regarded. A boy should not enter into conversation with a man, nor a gentleman with a lady, beyond some slight civility, without due encouragement. When persons meet on equal terms, in a railway carriage, at the sea side, or wherever accident may throw them together, although there should be no intrusion, there may be and ought to be, on the part of every one, a frank, kindly, neighbourly readiness to help each other by word and deed.

Very pleasant acquaintances are made, and lifelong friendships are sometimes the result of pleasant, friendly, and genial manners among fellow ravellers. The habitual reserve of most English people is senseless and cruel.

All our conduct to our fellow men should show our respect for them, our regard for their rights, our desire for their happiness. The first element of good manners is unselfishness. The moment a man thinks too much of himself, his own rights, his own happiness, he begins to be rude to others. The more entirely one devotes himself to securing the comfort and happiness of all around him, the better will be his manners, and good manners are 'twice blessed'. As the principle of all good conduct in society is the love of the neighbour, and an active philanthropy, so the element of all evil is egotism, selfishness, or the desire of one's own good and happiness, without regard to the rights and welfare of others. Thus, manners must be based on morals, and minor morals and major are substantially the same.

Haughty manners are the language of pride; cold manners, of indifference to the comfort and happiness of others; rude manners show a want of respect for the feelings of others;

scornful manners are a disregard of their rights; cynical and hypocritical manners are selfish and bad; good manners are the expression of good feeling, grace, delicacy, and refinement, free from pride, selfishness, or vanity.

A noble manner comes from a generous disposition – a heroic desire to sacrifice one's-self for the good of others. Genuine politeness shows itself to the poor and humble. A true gentleman is especially kind to the aged, the infirm, the unattractive; to those least likely to receive attentions from people who are only seeking their own pleasure.

Cheerfulness comes from health and hope. Animal spirits make us cheerful in the enjoyment of life and its sensations, but hope and charity give a spiritual cheerfulness, and even gayety of manner, which is very delightful. As far as possible, we should never show gloom or melancholy to those around us. If we carefully conceal what is unpleasant in our bodies, we should do no less with our humours or dispositions. We should never let it be seen that we are angry, cross, peevish, or low-spirited, where such mental states can give disquiet or pain to others. But the best way is never to be angry, cross, peevish, fretful, or disagreeable. That one should feel a flush of anger at injustice or rudeness; that one should be indignant at insult or outrage is natural – but in most cases there should be no violent expression of anger and indignation. We must never forget ourselves and what is due to our own character and dignity. There should always be in our own feeling and expression more of sorrow than of anger; and we must be ready to forgive every injury, as we hope to be forgiven.

A serene gayety, a courageous meeting of all the troubles and trials of life, is supremely good conduct and good manners. Calmness, patience, the firm possession of one's-self, are great virtues, but triumphant serenity or joyousness is more. And it is an emphatic precept of religion: 'Rejoice always; again I say rejoice.' This is the triumph of the higher sentiments of faith and hope over the lower feelings of distrust, grief, and anger. But a man may train himself in good feeling and good conduct as readily as he can avoid being round shouldered. It wants but a resolute will to secure either bodily or spiritual uprightness.

Every human being should do his part – whatever he is best able to do, in the work of life. An idle man or woman is a burden on industry; and generally worse than a burden. Certainly it is not polite to live on the labour of others without rendering some equivalent. Doubtless there are people who are ornaments to society, but has any one the right to be merely an ornament? Can one fairly claim a living in the world who only amuses himself and does no good to others? These are serious questions. If those who do the world's work, and provide all the necessaries of life, are content to feed, clothe, and shelter persons who are merely ornamental – pretty to look at – it is their own affair, but it seems to me a point of honour that everyone should do something for his daily bread, and not be willing to live upon the labour of others, without rendering some equivalent service. No one grudges pay for useful work, or for ornamental work, which is only another kind of use. We cheerfully pay the authors of any book we care to read, or the painter of any picture we care to see, but we do not so cheerfully give a portion of our hardly earned money to support people in idleness who do us no good and give us no pleasure. We bear patiently what is, not seeing the way to mend it; but if any of us were to go to work to organise a new society, should we find any place in it for people who would live upon our industry and render no service in return? And what shall be thought of the idle man who takes ten or twenty more from every kind of useful work to wait upon him – when all must be fed and clothed by those who work? But these are matters, you think, rather of morals and political economy, than of manners. I am not sure of that. It must be bad manners to pick a man's pocket in any way, or to add to the burthen of labour, or the oppression of the poor. But there will be no question that to be disorderly in one's life; to be unpunctual; not to keep promises or fulfil engagements; or pay one's debts, is very bad manners. A gentleman should be orderly in the smallest matters, mindful of all promises, duties, and engagements; always prompt, always punctual; never disappointing or vexing another by his neglect. A gentleman is one who can be depended upon to do what is right and just. Every debt is a debt of honour. Every engagement is sacred. You are sure that he speaks the truth. You know that he will keep his promise if it be possible. His word is as good as his bond; and he will do what he sees to be right in every case whatever may be the law about it. Upright and downright, pure equity governs all his actions. You can trust him utterly.

In all our relations to others, and our intercourse with them, we should try to enter into their views and feelings, and see things from their standpoint, 'Put yourself in his place.' Treat a servant as you would wish a master or mistress to treat you. If you would have friends, be friendly. Be at your ease in simple self-possession, and put others at their ease by accommodating yourself as far as you can to their manners. If George IV did pour his tea into his saucer when he was taking tea with some old ladies who followed that fashion, he showed that he had some claim to be called the first gentleman in Europe. A wise conformity in little things is far better than the assertion of an insolent superiority. A delicate regard for the feelings of others is the essence of politeness.

With a person of thoroughly good manners we are always at our ease. If we speak we are sure of being listened to with attention and sympathy. If we have a favour to ask the way is made easy. If granted, it is done so graciously as to double its value; if refused, it is so kindly done that we scarcely regret it, and feel sure that the refusal was prompted by the best motives. We meet such a person with pleasure, and part with real regret. A sunshine of geniality gives warmth and pleasantness to all about him. He may not have wit, but he has a worth far greater. He has the secret of happiness – the power of making everyone he meets more content with life, more resigned to its trials, more happy in its enjoyments.

ACCOMPLISHMENTS

The first and highest of human accomplishments is a clear, distinct, well-modulated speech. A child learning to talk should have good teachers. It is as easy to learn a refined and elegant way of speaking as a coarse and awkward way. Even purity and delicacy of tone may be in some degree acquired. Children are very imitative. They copy as closely as they can the sounds they hear. If parents, nurses, and teachers were nice and careful in their speech, children would follow their example.

The tone of the voice indicates character; the mode of speaking shows training and education. We never get a proper idea of man or woman until we have heard them speak. A vulgar man may pass undetected if quiet and well dressed, but his speech will betray him. The ear is a better judge of character and breeding than the eye.

The tone of voice depends upon the firmness or delicacy of the organs of speech. There are vocal organs of wonderful flexibility and beauty – tones that enchant all who hear them. But every voice may be improved by careful culture, not only in childhood and youth, but at every age.

Articulation is still more a matter of imitation or art. Every sound should be deliberately and carefully formed, without drawling, without slovenliness, without affectation. Every word should be neatly pronounced in the best way – the manner used by the most cultivated people. In English there is no other rule. See that the aspirates are rightly placed; see that the r's are properly sounded, neither too little nor too much; see that the proper syllables are accented; see that the tones are modulated musically and sensibly as well; that the right words are emphasised; that each member of a sentence has the right inflection. Follow the best models you can hear. Speak simply, in short, familiar Saxon words. Speak colloquially, and not in the stilted language of many books. Speak naturally, and so as to express easily and accurately every thought and feeling. Clearness and accuracy of speech consist in the use of the right words placed in the most simple grammatical relations, without complexity or obscurity of meaning. We must use the right word in the right place. Style is picturesque in its allusions, and musical in rhythm or cadences. But in both speech and writing we must avoid the inflated, the turgid, the bombastic. Simplicity is the rule of good taste, in language as in manner. The author of *Realmah* says,

> A weighty sentence should be powerful in its substantives, choice and discreet in its adjectives, nicely correct in its verbs: not a word that could be added, nor one which the most fastidious would venture to suppress: in order, lucid; in sequence, logical; in method, perspicuous, and yet with a pleasant and inviting intricacy which disappears as you advance: the language, not quaint, not obsolete, not common, and not new; its several clauses justly proportioned and carefully balanced, so that it moves like a well-disciplined army organised for conquest; the rhythm, not that of music, but of a higher and more fantastic melodiousness, submitting to no rule, incapable of being taught: the substance and form alike disclosing a happy union of the soul of the author to the subject of his thought: having, therefore, individuality without personal predominance; and, withal, there must be a sense of felicity about it, declaring it to be the product of a happy moment, so that you feel that it will not happen again to that man who writes the sentence, or to any other of the sons of men, to say the like thing so choicely, tersely, melifluously, and completely.

Speak so distinctly as to be readily heard and understood by those you address, and by all you wish to hear you. It need not usually be loud. Even the partially deaf hear better a low, distinct speech, than a loud one less carefully articulate.

Avoid, or if you have fallen into the habit speedily amend it, all mumbling and muttering. Speak so clearly that no one can have any excuse for not distinguishing your words. Stammering and stuttering both come from trying to speak too quickly. Any stutterer or stammerer can sing, because he has to utter the syllables one by one, each in its own time. Let him speak each syllable by itself, resting a little on the vowels, and he will soon be cured.

Avoid the English fashion of making meaningless sounds between the words – of saying 'er, er, er', and humming and hawing. It is true that Sir Robert Peel had such a habit, and set the fashion which so many have followed; but it is not a sensible or beautiful one, and the sooner such a fashion is changed the better. If a man cannot remember the word he wants, he does not help the matter by making a succession of unmeaning and unpleasant noises.

A worse habit, because it has even a sillier seeming, is that of laughing when one speaks. It is not easy to tell a funny story without at the same time laughing at the fun, and some can do it without spoiling the story; but this is different from an insane giggle bursting out with every sentence, even when there is no joke about it. Most drolleries come best from a sober face.

For accent read poetry and consult the dictionaries. But one who associates with educated people can rarely go amiss; and so of pronunciation. It is hard to avoid provincialisms of speech in a country where the language of the common people in several counties can scarcely be understood by those who merely speak English. But educated men, especially university men, everywhere speak much alike, though the purest English is said to be spoken in Dublin. But as a rule, Irishmen, Scotchmen, Welshmen, and the people of Yorkshire, Lancashire, Lincolnshire, Somersetshire, &c., can readily be distinguished by their speech. So can nearly all Americans – but more by the tones of their voices than any peculiarity of pronunciation, as, for some reason, they speak in a sharp, contracted, nasal tone, while the English sounds are broader and more gutteral, and French and Italian still more open. The French have certain sounds called nasal; but with most Americans all the sounds have that character.

How it is that so many English, not only Cockneys, but people living in all parts of England, manage not only to drop their h's, but to put them wherever they do not belong, however difficult it may be, and why the absurd and perverse fashion should be kept up from generation to generation, no philosopher has explained. Compulsory education may mend the matter – but who began it, and why? Of course everyone who imagines that he may be shaky about his aspirates, should put himself in training at once to get them into the right places. To do this, resolutely read aloud, at first, if need be, with a friendly critic. Practice, I have no doubt, will overcome the evil habit, but in any excitement there is always danger of a relapse.

Next to a pure and beautiful speech, reading aloud is the most useful and delightful accomplishment. It seems as if every good speaker ought to be also a good reader, but it is not so at all. A man who converses easily, who tells a story with animation, who has no fault of tone, pronunciation, emphasis, or inflection in his speech, may be the most humdrum and monotonous of readers. Not one clergyman in ten can read the service and sermons tolerably. The scarcity of good readers is very surprising. Even of those who make a business of reading in public, three out of four read very badly. Charles Dickens read the introductions monotonously, but when he came to the story, his readings were very dramatic and effective. Fanny Kemble is a royal reader – one of the very best; but most public readings are more a pain than a pleasure to hear.

I cannot tell why it should be so, since to speak well, and to read as well as one speaks, seem to be perfectly easy and natural. Why should clergymen, with a thorough education and constant practice in reading the finest things in the language, read badly in so many cases? Lawyers both speak and read better – I think because they are more in earnest. They want to convince court or jury, and go at it with a will.

The rule of right reading, when one has a good voice and good pronunciation, is to read just as one would speak. If a man thoroughly understands his author, and can make the words, his own, and utter them just as he would in talking when quite in earnest, he reads well. Here is the difficulty. With most people reading is a mechanical and monotonous task which has in it none of the inflections, graces, force, or animation of speech. How to learn? Read alone as if you were talking. Commit colloquial writing to memory, then speak it. Read to children, trying to make them understand what you read. Resolutely throw off the constraint of print, and read as you would speak. I know no other way.

Another useful accomplishment is that of a clear, legible, good handwriting. If it can be strong, graceful, and full of character and high breeding, so much the better. But only decent care is needed to make it as legible as print. Only decent care, and yet how many handwritings are so difficult to read that we are tempted to lay important letters aside and never read them.

The best model to follow in writing is the ordinary italic print. With some modification of the capital letters, it is pretty enough, and very easy to read. When one has acquired a legible hand, it will gradually shape itself into all of character and gracefulness one can put into it. The writing of women in this country is far worse than that of the men. Nearly all are taught the same stiff, angular, graceless hand. It is a fashion – I do not know its origin, but wish that, like other fashions, it would change. I get hundreds of letters from ladies all so alike that I can scarcely tell them apart – differing chiefly in degrees of cramped ungracefulness and illegibility. None of this writing is good, and the worst is very ugly. I have scarcely seen a really beautiful and characteristic feminine handwriting in England. Yet what a lovely accomplishment it is! – for such a hand as a lady ought to write, is a perpetual delight.

Music is a talent, and everyone who has it ought to cultivate and use it for his own pleasure and the delight of others. Everyone can speak, read, and write in some fashion, but only those who have an ear for music can play, and only those who have both ear and voice can sing. To sing well requires the same kind of taste and feeling that are required to make a good speaker or reader.

It is a great mistake to think that everyone can be taught to play or sing. With great pains a person without a musical ear may be taught to play mechanically on the pianoforte or other keyed instrument, but never on the violin, or to sing, and all efforts to teach those who have not ear or voice are worse than wasted. Singers and musicians are like poets – born, not made. If the talent comes out spontaneously, give it opportunity for development. It wants little more.

The same may be said of drawing, painting, and all artistic accomplishments. They are gifts to be thankful for and made use of. It is a waste of time, effort, and money to try to teach them where the genius or special talent does not exist.

It is well for everyone to learn to dance, to learn to fence, perhaps to box, to practice gymnastics. The latter are of great use to many of both sexes, whose bodies need orderly exercise. They all give strength, grace, and presence of mind, and enable one to carry one's self to better advantage. All of them make men more manly, and some at least make women more womanly. It may be a question of good taste or of morals whether ladies should dance this or that style of dances at balls, but it can harm no child to learn to turn out his toes, to bow gracefully, to carry himself well, and enter or leave a room with propriety. The earlier good habits of this sort are learned the better. I would have, in every school, half an hour every day devoted to military drill, and another half hour to dancing. In London the poorest children learn to dance. At the sound of the hand-organ, they assemble in every dingy square and dance like mad as long as the music lasts. These are the bright and happy hours of lives that do not see too many.

Children, from three years old to seven, learn languages with a wonderful facility. There seems something magical in the rapidity with which they learn to talk, and so active is the memory of words in early years that a child will learn three or four languages as easily as one. Later in life the acquisition of a foreign tongue becomes more difficult, and it is much more difficult with some than with others. Acquiring languages easily is a special gift. Some have been able to speak forty languages, and been able to acquire enough of one for conversation in a few hours. Others work wearily for months. Most persons, however, can learn to speak French, German, or Italian, when it becomes a matter of necessity. Go where you can hear nothing else, and where you must speak that or nothing, and you soon learn. If you mean to travel, by all means learn the language of every country you propose to visit – enough, at least, for ordinary uses.

Every well educated person indeed should learn, as thoroughly as he can, four languages – two dead; two living; besides his own. He should know Latin and Greek, French and German. The former are the keys of literature and science; the English language is largely composed of words deriving from them. French is the language of courts and society. German is a storehouse of literature and philosophy. Italian is the language of music and art. To well learn any language is in itself a liberal education. Above all, a man should thoroughly master his own, and he can do this only by a careful, thoughtful reading of its best writers, and an equally scrupulous avoidance of its worst.

'Evil communications corrupt good manners.'

SOCIETY

Society is a word of large and various meaning. We talk of being in society, the interests of society, a good position in society, fashionable society, general society. It is properly the friendly meeting of people together to enjoy conversation and amusement with each other. To enjoy society, mutual protection, help, and to be amused with each other, men gather in villages and towns. Meeting often, they find the necessity of making themselves agreeable to each other. They refrain from offensive or injurious conduct, and they find frequent occasions for mutual civilities and reciprocal good offices. To live pleasantly with each other, men must abandon, or at least conceal, selfishness, injustice, evil tempers, dishonesty, falsehood, and every mean and annoying disposition, and become, or at least appear to be, kind, friendly, disinterested, obliging, cheerful, honest, and honourable. Contact rounds off the rough edges of character, and gives polish to the manners. Politeness, civility, and urbanity mean the manners of people who live in cities.

In a large sense, every person is considered a member of society; but we speak of a solitary person as one who goes into no society – meaning one who neither visits nor is visited. A disreputable person is not admitted into society. A morose person shuns society. A person of loose habits and associations mingles in low society.

What is this low society? In one sense it is immoral, made up of persons who disregard the observances and moralities of the social standard. It is people who are poor; who do not dress well; who live in unfashionable neighbourhoods, or follow unfashionable employments; who lack cultivation, manner, taste, birth, or whatever is held to be necessary to good society. Where a hereditary aristocracy rules, a man's social position depends upon his ancestors. Of such men it has sometimes been said that the best part of them is under ground; but no one can deny the advantages of birth and breeding. Wealth gives the means and conditions of the highest culture. We have breeds of men as distinctly marked as our breeds of dogs and horses, and men are born with noble, heroic, and beautiful qualities as they are with unfortunate and base ones. We speak rightly of born liars and born thieves. There is, therefore, an aristocracy of birth, and to be well born is a great good fortune. But this kind of aristocracy is not always that of rank, title, or wealth. The child of healthy, honest, educated and refined parents is well born and a true aristocrat.

High society is composed of people of rank or wealth, who are able to live in a certain style of luxury and splendour; who can give elegant dinners and balls, and assemble around them people of taste and fashion. Good society is composed of good, friendly, intelligent, tasteful people, who can benefit, interest, and amuse each other.

Everywhere in society ladies have precedence and honour. They are to have the first seats and the best seats. No gentleman can be seated while a lady stands. No gentleman can help himself to anything until ladies are helped. It is a principle of society that women are to be everywhere deferred to, protected, esteemed, and honoured. In the rudest regions of America when, not only a lady, but any woman enters a railway carriage, some man rises to give her a seat. On a Mississippi steamboat, no man is allowed to sit down at the table until every woman is seated. Front seats at public entertainments are the same price as back ones, but they are reserved for ladies and when all passengers pay the same price, the most elegant carriages are, by common consent, also reserved for ladies – that is, for all females and their attendants. The same rule prevails in hotels and everywhere. More deference is shown to women, as women, in America than in any country in the world.

Over all social festivities the lady of the house presides. She receives calls, gives invitations, welcomes the guests, sits at the head of the table, and is the social queen. The husband devotes himself to the ladies, and generally to the comfort of the guests.

To enter a society to which one is a stranger, some introduction is required. Going to a strange district, one carries letters of introduction. A man presents you to his friend, and vouches for your social position and good conduct. He introduces you to others. The Texan gentleman had a very proper idea of the responsibilities of an introduction when he said – 'Mr A., this is my friend Mr B.; if he steals anything, I'm responsible.' But such social endorsement, whether by word or letter, should not be lightly given. A man may not pick your pocket, but he may be a bore, and steal your time and patience. You do not wish to make the acquaintance of a man who will ever annoy or injure you – one whom you cannot trust in every way.

But there are cases in which no introductions are required. People thrown casually together, as at hotels, in watering places, and generally in travelling, can always make modest advances towards such temporary acquaintance as the circumstances warrant. A satirical poet has represented two Englishmen cast away on a desert island, refusing to speak to each other because they had not been introduced. It is not so bad as that. I have found a gentleman silent from London to Oxford, yet civil before coming to Evesham, and cordially shaking hands when parting at Malvern, after a delightful conversation.

The two classes who most readily enter into conversation are those whose positions are assured, so that they have no trouble about them – the higher and the lower. A nobleman will enter readily into conversation with any one, sure that he will not compromise his dignity, just as he will carry a parcel, or wheel a barrow, if he has occasion to do so. The common people are always as courteous as they know how to be. It is in the middle class where people are always in trouble for fear they may lower themselves, that we find any difficulty. The more entirely a man is a gentleman, and the woman a lady, the more they are at their ease, and disposed to be kind, courteous, and considerate of all around them. It is a quality of true nobility that it 'condescends to men of low estate'.

No introductions are needed between people invited to a dinner, or tea, party or assembly of any kind. The fact that two persons are the guests of a mutual acquaintance is an introduction to each other. You have a right to offer a civility, or the charm of your society, to any lady present. You can ask any one to dance. You can enter into conversation.

In society all selfishness must be laid aside; all exclusiveness is in bad taste. Affianced lovers must not be noticeably attentive to each other, and husbands and wives are seldom seen together. A gentleman never dances with his wife, and never takes her down to dinner. Good taste, politeness, and a regard for the rights and feelings of others, require that we refrain in society from the assertion or manifestation of any exclusive right or privilege.

It is for this reason that a man does not eat or drink without asking his neighbour to partake. It is for this reason that you never open and read a letter in company without the apology of asking permission. It is for this reason that all fondlings and familiarities before company are improper. You have no right to do anything which any other person has not an equal right to do, with the lady's permission. The assertion, therefore, of any exclusive right to the caresses of your wife or mistress, in the presence of others, is a gross indelicacy. Consequently, every appearance of this kind is carefully avoided. At table, husband and wife sit as far as possible from each other, and, at balls, husbands and wives are separated and take other partners. Society is the enlargement, the absorption, and, for the time being, the breaking up of all private and exclusive engagements. For a similar reason, tête-à-têtes, or the private conversation of two persons, exclusive and long continued, should be avoided. There are opportunities enough for private love-making, courtship, &c. If a gentleman wishes to see a lady alone, let him make a special visit for that purpose; but in public, all talents, all charms, all the intelligence, and wit, and sentiment of conversation – all the graces and accomplishments are the property of all, or at least of the group of those who are attracted to each other by similarity and sympathy.

As a rule, men and women should meet together in society. The influence of men upon each other, when left to themselves in clubs or at the dinner table, is not of a very refining character; and women, when left to themselves, are said to indulge too freely in tittle tattle and scandal.

Each sex has a restraining and elevating influence upon the other. Society is, properly speaking, therefore, the mingling of both, and assemblages which are all male or all female are not society. And in a social assemblage, every group, when it is large enough to break into groups, should be composed of both sexes.

In America, where social experiments are more freely and boldly tried than in Europe, there are colleges where young people of both sexes are educated together; living in the same boarding houses, eating at the same tables, and reciting in the same classes; and the result, I am assured, has been admirable in its influence upon both. The young men have been made more manly, and the young women more womanly by the influence of each sex upon the other.

There should also be, I think, in all society, a considerable variety of ages. The model of a true society is a family of three generations. The unnatural hours of fashionable assemblies make them unsuitable for children; but I see no reason why boys and girls of fifteen, and all ages from that to a hundred or more, may not mingle in social gatherings. The very old enjoy the company of the very young. I have seen three generations dancing in one set in a quadrille. But as no one should go into society who cannot in some way contribute to its enjoyments, the age at which one may be admitted must depend upon fitness in manners and acquirements.

All persons in society are equal. In conversation and in amusements all distinctions are laid aside. The sole exception to this is when a procession is formed from the drawing room to the dinner-table; when the lady of the house takes the arm of the gentleman who is the most distinguished guest or greatest stranger, and the host offers his, next in order, to the most distinguished lady, or greatest stranger, and then all march down in the order of their rank or social position. But, once returned to the drawing-room, all this is laid aside, and the only distinction is the power to please. A beautiful and accomplished lady is queen; the most elegant and interesting man is the centre of attraction. A brilliant commoner is better than a dull duke. By common consent, society lays aside artificial distinctions, and attends only to natural and acquired advantages, to character, genius, and manners.

What we want for the enjoyment of society is the intelligence that qualifies us for conversation; the wit that makes us entertaining; the tact, delicacy, and regard for the feelings of others which will preserve us from doing or saying anything which can hurt or offend them; the amiability or kindness of disposition which will make us seek to make everybody about us happy, and the presence of mind, or possession of ourselves, which will allow us to say and do everything in the best manner. The more we can dismiss self, the less we have of self-consciousness, and the idea that everybody is concerned about us – the more we are occupied with everybody and everything but ourselves, the better for our social success.

As women are the queens of society – as there can be no society, properly speaking, without them – as they are its one attraction and perpetual charm, everything depends upon their fitness for its duties and requirements. A vulgar or silly woman, an awkward or ill-tempered one, makes society with her impossible. Happily such women are rare. Most women have the gifts of grace and amiability. They are the natural centres around which the best elements of social life spontaneously gather. And in spite of fashionable follies and frivolities, women every day become more brave, self-reliant, free, noble, and in a word, womanly. Every day there is less oppression of the physically weaker, but morally stronger sex – stronger by influence, if not by character; and, with universal education, the time cannot be distant when women in England will be entirely relieved from the coarse and heavy work of coal pits and brickfields, and when the beating of wives, and cruel treatment of female children, will only be known in the history of a barbarous past.

But there is nothing unwomanly or unladylike in every woman being industriously and usefully employed. Every woman ought to be able to make her own clothing, and the clothing of at least young children. Every woman ought to know how to cook, so as to prepare a good meal in case of need, and to teach and direct her servants. She should be able to do everything that makes a house comfortable and elegant. Once every lady, the highest in the land, could make bread, and spin, and weave, as well as sew and embroider, and women have not gained in character, nor the country in prosperity, by depriving women of nearly all kinds of domestic work, and removing so many useful and beautiful arts from the household to the factory. Women have lost many useful avocations, and are now crying out for others. Netting, crochet, and fancy work do not satisfy them. Dressing and making calls is not a business for life. Only a few have the gifts which qualify them to be artists and authors.

The lack of sensible and useful employments drives women into unladylike and immoral practices. They must do something. A young lady, full of health and animal spirits, cannot spend all her time in reading novels. She is driven to dissipation and flirtation. What she reads so much about in the three volume sets from Mudie's she wishes to experience. She preserves her reputation, no doubt, but what becomes of her character? And, in the absence of other interests, there comes to many young women the feverish desire for marriage and a settlement in life – a thing which should never rest in her thoughts. It spoils the charm of any woman to be thinking of a possible husband. Match-making mamma's are bad enough – husband-hunting girls are intolerable. They repel more than they attract. A woman is never so charming as in utter unconsciousness of charm – never so attractive as when she has no thought of attracting. In society, all possibilities of future relations should be kept out of sight, and every one treated according to his merits. In fact, marriage, actual or possible, should be utterly ignored. Men and women in society do not meet as husbands and wives, or lovers and mistresses – only as members of society, in unrestrained freedom to make themselves agreeable to each other. An evident flirtation with any one is a rudeness to all the rest of the company. Special attentions are in bad taste, and sure to offend. And when a lady feels that she has made the impression she most wished to make on the man she desired to attract and charm, because she felt his worth, though her heart may bound with happiness, she must no more show it than she can show the antipathies and disgusts excited by others.

A true-hearted woman, with a fair amount of culture, a person not disagreeable, with some taste and observation of life, and a warm benevolence, and desire to please, can scarcely fail to make herself an agreeable and welcome guest in every circle. But a false, uncultured one, with no taste or care for pleasing, critical and censorious, jealous and malicious, is one of the worst samples of the feminine part of humanity.

A lady of taste, refinement, and with so much of wealth and fashion as to give her a certain position in society, may become the centre of a circle, a social pivot, an educator, and in many ways a benefactor. Her furniture, the order of her apartments, her pictures and statuary, her own dress and ornaments, may be such as to give pleasure and improvement to every person who visits her. Why should not her boudoir or drawing-room be as nicely arranged, and as pretty a study in art, as any picture? Is she not herself, in the possibilities of her air, and manner, in pose and gesture, in dress and ornament, a work of art, as she may be much more in feeling and expression? Her sphere is to cheer, to refine, to beautify, and bless. The opportunities and influence she may thus acquire, she may turn to the noblest and holiest purposes. You make a call of ten minutes on such a woman, and she lives in your mind and heart a picture of beauty, grace, and charm, for long years after. Her dress, her air, her sweet, engaging manner, the few well-chosen words of genial politeness, the melody of her voice, the kind glances of her pure and tender eyes, the gentle pressure of her soft hand, all thrill in pleasant memories.

The rules of fashion with respect to women are in some respects very absurd. A young unmarried lady must always be accompanied by her mother, chaperon, or some kind of protector. She is really as closely guarded as in Turkey, though not in the same way. 'A young married lady cannot present herself in public without the protection of the husband, or an aged lady,' so says fashion. If fashion condescended to give a reason, it would be that no young woman can be trusted with her own virtue or reputation. 'They are at liberty' – we quote again – 'to walk with young married ladies, or unmarried ones, while the latter should never walk alone with their companions.' Young ladies are not even to be trusted with each other. 'Neither should they show themselves, except with a gentleman of their family, and then he should be a near relation, of *respectable age*!' 'Young widows have equal liberty with married ladies.'

If we may be permitted to make a suggestion, it is that wives, widows, and young ladies are much better able to take care of themselves, and much more to be trusted, than these rules would indicate. They smack of the seraglio; they are but one step from prisons and eunuchs; they are an insult to female intelligence and female virtue.

Why not say a married man can only walk out with his wife or some elderly person of his own sex? Young gentlemen should never walk alone with their companions; neither should they show themselves except with a lady of their family, and then she should be a near relation, of respectable age – a great aunt or grandmother!

In large towns, and wherever there may be ruffians to insult and even assault her, every woman should have protection. In well lighted, frequented, and especially business streets, there is little or no danger. The rules quoted seem intended to guard a woman against herself. A virtuous woman does not need them.

ETIQUETTE

The word etiquette means a ticket, and the ceremonies of special occasions were formerly written on cards or tickets, furnished to each person who took part in them. Such cards are still delivered, in some places, to the mourners at funerals, and we have bills of fare at dinners, the order of dancing at balls, and programmes at entertainments. So cards of invitation tell us that there is to be dancing, and cards of admission sometimes specify what dress is to be worn. Thus, evening dress is required at the opera, and in some cases at church, as in the chapels of Royal Palaces. Chambers' *Encyclopaedia* says,

> Popular publications are constantly issuing from the press for the purpose of teaching etiquette, or the rules of behaviour in good society. They will, for the most part, be found far less trustworthy than the promptings of nature, where the individual possesses a reasonable amount of reverence for others, and respect for himself. Yet there are certain conventionalities which can only be learned by instruction of some kind, or by observation, and the observation may be attended by unpleasant circumstances.

It is quite true that all our manners and observances are, or should be, founded on a common sense of propriety, of the duty we owe to others, and a proper regard for the comfort and happiness of all around us. The best and cleverest people behave to others in certain ways, and we observe, admire and imitate them. There are fashions of manners as of dress, but they are much less changeable. In the East, every act of one's life has been reduced to rule and system, and the etiquette of China and Japan has lasted, with little change, for ages. Every one learns all that will ever be required of him in his conduct to superiors, equals, and inferiors, and in every relation of life. In the West, we are left more free, and there is more individuality and originality; but with them we have also more that is disorderly and offensive. It is one of the great discomforts of social life not to know what is the right thing to do, what is expected of you, and how you can make yourself agreeable, or, at least, not disagreeable to those around you. We feel 'at home' wherever we know how to conduct ourselves. Bashfulness, timidity, awkwardness, and all the confusion and suffering that they cause, come from not knowing how to behave. The moment we know what we ought to say and do, everything is easy and delightful. A sensitive mind fears nothing so much as being blundering and ridiculous. There are few of us who are quite free of some dread of 'Mrs Grundy.'

Education in etiquette begins very early. The mother trains the child from its earliest years – the child imitates its parents. Children are continually warned that this is not nice, and that that is not proper. A child brought up by and among well-behaved people, can hardly go amiss unless from natural perversity. The misfortune is, that nurses, servants, and even teachers are taken from the lower ranks of life, and in many cases have no aptitude for good manners or no instruction. If servants were selected for their good manners; if they were required among the qualifications of teachers, the demand would create the supply. Observation and imitation would be stimulated if good manners were the condition of success in life.

But there is wanting, first of all, the desire, and then the perception of deferent and refined behaviour, and of its two elements, self-respect, and respect for others – true self-love and the love of the neighbour. The stolid indifference to all decent manners we see about us, comes from a want of sense of their importance, much more, I believe, than from a brutal disregard of what is right. When workmen stand upon the sidewalk, so as to oblige women to step into the gutter to get past them, it is charitable to think they are muddled with beer. When people crowd and crush you, and make mad rushes to get the best positions, violating every principle of decent manners, it seems like innate depravity – but it is, perhaps, only a bad habit which they have thoughtlessly drifted into. And this exhibition of brutal selfishness is not confined to the lower ranks of life. The crowding and confusion are sometimes as great in the palace of the sovereign as at the pit entrance of a theatre. When George IV left Carleton House the fashionable world was admitted to see its splendours. The result was a crowd in which ladies were crushed, trampled upon, and in some cases their clothes entirely torn from their bruised bodies. Such manners are what we might expect in a horde of savages. Surely they are not such as we look for among an enlightened and Christian people.

If the manners of the upper and middle classes were more gentle, refined, polished, courteous, and Christian, they would have their influence upon the lower class in their behaviour to each other, and especially to women and children, and even to dumb animals; and our newspapers would not be filled with the details of violence and cruelty – men horribly beating, and often murdering, their wives and little ones. It is the disgrace of the aristocracy of any country when any portion of its lower classes are ignorant, drunken, and infuriated savages. They are responsible for it by their example or their neglect. What is the use of a noble lord if he cannot instruct and influence those about him? A nobleman is a civiliser – he has no other *raison d'étre*. The lower classes of the English people are drunken, because there was once in England such a saying as 'drunk as a lord'. If aristocrats kill horses in fox hunts and steeple chases, is it wonderful that colliers should have dog fights, or costermongers beat donkeys? The lower classes copy the manners and morals of the higher, and the sooner the wealthy and educated people of England become humane in their pastimes, and kind and gentle in their behaviour, the sooner will a true civilisation spread through all classes. A virtuous sovereign diffuses the love of virtue among millions. A dissolute one is an unspeakable misfortune. And so in degree of every person whose position, wealth, or social importance of any kind, gives him social influence.

The little observances of social life are more important than many people think them. The outward signs or expressions of any sentiment not only manifest it to others, but help to keep it active in ourselves. This is the use of all ceremony and ritualism in religion. We strengthen our own reverence by external expressions, and help to excite it in others. A great assembly kneeling with bowed heads in prayer, or uniting in songs of fervent praise, is very impressive. And the same principle governs all social ceremonies and observances.

Salutations are social ceremonies. A gentleman raises his hat as a mark of respect; he touches it to intimates; he takes it off to ladies, and when he stops to speak to them, or to persons to whom he wishes to show a marked deference, he does not put it on till requested to do so. The hat is touched or raised with the hand farthest from the person saluted.

We do not salute a friend who is engaged with a lady or a person superior in rank whom we do not know; but we join a friend in returning the salutation of a stranger to ourself. It is the right of a lady to recognise an acquaintance or not at her pleasure; and unless very intimate, a gentleman waits for such recognition. So of stopping for conversation. If we wish to converse more than a few moments, it is better to turn and walk with the one we meet. But a lady or superior must give the invitation. In passing persons frequently, you are not to salute every time. Once is sufficient.

Visitors – if strangers – we meet according to rank, position, or intimacy. A gentleman meets a lady at the front door, and accompanies her to the sidewalk, or puts her into the carriage, at her departure; and the same with any person to whom he wishes to show particular consideration. A lady receives in her drawing-room, and does not leave it for gentlemen unless age or position call for special deference. Ladies treat ladies as gentlemen do each other. The visitor salutes his hostess first and last. The manner in which we salute all persons should express the respect and kindness we feel for them, or ought to feel, and which they ought to merit. By treating every one with courtesy we in fact demand of them the character and manners which merit our respect. We, in this way, put everybody on his good behaviour. A polite man is thus not only a teacher of politeness, but a practical reformer of manners and morals. The place of honour in a room is the farthest from the entrance – at a fireside, the corners; at table, the right of the hostess and host.

Introductions are a convenient mode of making people acquainted with each other. The one who introduces becomes responsible for the good behaviour of both. No one ought to introduce to another a man who will insult or swindle, annoy or injure him. There are special introductions only for particular objects. At a ball a gentleman is introduced to a lady simply as her partner for a dance. She is not required to recognise him again. In merely formal introductions people bow to each other, but do not shake hands. Hand shaking should be the sign of a friendly intimacy. When a lady gives her hand to a gentleman, it should mean that she accepts his friendship. The Americans shake hands everywhere and with everybody. There is abundant hand shaking among the Germans. The English and French are more properly reticent. It is for the person to whom one is introduced to offer or withhold his hand.

As a rule, introductions should not be given except at the request or with the permission expressed or understood of the persons introduced; but intimate friends of both parties may presume upon its being desirable and agreeable. The inferior in age or position is always introduced to the superior, and gentlemen to ladies, unless there is a marked difference in rank or age; but when equals are introduced the form is repeated, and so each introduced to the other.

A letter of introduction should be brief and confined to the matter in hand, and given unsealed to the bearer. If given for any purpose of business, you can call and send it in with your card. Otherwise send it with your card, and wait to have it acknowledged. If the letter is addressed to a lady, however, you must call, send it in, and of course give her time to read it.

Calls are very brief visits made in the morning, but the fashionable morning is any time before dinner. Morning calls should, however, never be made till sometime after lunch – say three o'clock, nor later than five; since people dine at from six to eight o'clock, and must have time to dress. Usually no call should last more than fifteen minutes, and when other visitors arrive, it may be shorter. As there is no obligation to see people, ladies who do not wish to seem rude tell their servants to say 'not at home' to those they decline to see. They may be indisposed or engaged, but 'not at home' is a formula which covers the whole ground, and is not to be taken literally. It may mean not 'at home' to you on this occasion; and to most callers it is a welcome announcement. They leave a card, which answers every purpose of a merely formal visit.

Even this matter might be simplified. In a certain German town it was once the custom for everybody to call upon all his acquaintances on new years. As the town grew this became such a burthen to callers and entertainers that they got to sending cards instead, which set all the servants in the town to running their feet off. Finally the servants took all the cards to a central place, where they were sorted over, and each one carried home those intended for his family, which is the present excellent time and labour-saving custom.

A call, or the card, its equivalent, must be returned within a week; and every entertainment, dinner, ball, to which you are invited, must be responded to by a call, if you desire another invitation. When about to be absent for some time, it is expected that you will make a farewell visit to your acquaintances. If you do not see them, leave your card with P. P. C. upon it – '*Pour prendre conge.*' On your return, you are entitled to receive the first visit.

When a clergyman comes to a new parish, he calls ex-officio upon every family in the place – upon the poorest first, upon the most wealthy and distinguished last, excepting the sick and afflicted, who of course have precedence over all others. These calls are not to be returned; the tax upon the clergyman's time would be too heavy. Should he be married, however, the ladies call upon his wife and welcome her with due respect to their society. Other professional men make calls, but they are more of a business than a social character.

Receptions are admirable inventions for economy and enjoyment. Instead of spending time in calls, or money in dinners, parties, balls, &c., a lady sends a card to all her friends to inform them that she is 'at home' on some evening once a week. If she manage her cards well, she may gather around her a delightful society. She has only to offer her visitors a cup of tea or coffee when they arrive, and a bit of cake or a sandwich and glass of wine later. No formal supper is expected. There is conversation and music. The more really at home the hostess is, the better for her visitors, who come early or late, and stay as short a time or as long as they like. It is obvious that there can be only here and there one who can have such evenings; and no lady can expect to fill her rooms week after week unless she has the tact to draw to her agreeable people, and, what is far more difficult, to order, regulate, and govern her guests, and banish bores, disagreeables, and incompatibles from her society.

At these receptions the less formality the better. Everyone is introduced already by the fact of his admission. If you know the lady hostess you know all her guests, and you can in no way please her so much as by making yourself agreeable to any and all of them, and especially to any who are, or who seem liable to be, neglected. As at your entrance you go and pay your respects to the lady of the house, so at your departure you very quietly take your leave of her at last, after having said a private good-bye to any others, and so vanish without disturbance. Neither in arriving or departing should a guest of any rank below royalty allow himself to make a sensation. Still, to all who must necessarily observe you, there must be some sign of courtesy. One should never enter or leave even an omnibus or railway compartment without some, if ever so slight, mark of respect.

In all cases where there is a set time of beginning, the highest etiquette is perfect punctuality. No one can dine until the last guest arrives. To keep people waiting, to make a dinner spoil, is more than an impoliteness – it is an outrage. So, at a theatre or concert, be in your place before the curtain rises, so as not to disturb the enjoyment of others; and never be so rude as to leave just before the play or concert ends. Leave at the end of the last act or piece of music but one, if you please; but to disturb an audience by going out at the very climax of interest is a very selfish piece of ill manners. But in almost all cases ill manners is some display of selfishness. Good manners consists in a consideration for the feelings and rights of others. What right have you to mar the enjoyment of music or a play by conversation? What right to stand up before people who are trying to see some spectacle? Every way in which you consult your own gratification at the expense of others is unmannerly and unjust. An honest man does what is right or equitable; a polite or courteous man goes always beyond this line, and high breeding is philanthropy. No man of gallantry would allow a lady to wait for him one moment; and simple honesty requires that everyone should be punctual in keeping engagements. To make sure one should be a few minutes before the time, at all events not an instant after. So every railway company should be held strictly to its time-tables. The minute of arrival and departure at every place is a part of its contract with every passenger.

And let us advise punctuality in going as well as in coming, and especially celerity in taking leave. If parting be a pain, do not make it wearisome as well. If we 'speed the parting guest', he should say goodbye, and go at once. It is not necessary to be rudely abrupt, but in saying goodbye, the sooner it is over the better for all concerned. Suspense is painful to the parties, and tiresome to spectators.

When two ride on horseback, one must ride behind. Precedence is a necessity, and when it is regulated, we avoid confusion. If everyone insisted upon being first and best, it would fill the world with quarrels. If we followed everywhere the Christian rule of taking the lowest place, in honour preferring one another, and seeking, not our own, but another's good, it would fill the world with peace. Think of carrying this rule into all our bargains and business! Everyone can see that practical Christianity would reform the world.

In all civilised countries, where distinctions of rank or position are recognised, there are some rules of precedence for occasions of state and ceremony. In England the order of precedence has been established by statutes, royal letters patent, and ancient usages. The constable and marshal in the Court of Chivalry settled the rank and place of every one. Persons of the same rank follow each other in the order of the creation of that rank. In the English peerage the younger sons of each preceding rank take place after the eldest son of the next succeeding rank. Married women and widows take the same rank among each other as their husbands, unless such rank be professional or official – but no office gives rank to wife or children. Unmarried women rank with their eldest brother; but the wife of the eldest son precedes her husband's sisters, and all other ladies of the same degree. Marriage with an inferior does not take away a lady's rank.

The tables of precedence among men and among women in England would fill several pages. The first begins with the Sovereign, the Prince of Wales, sons of the Sovereign, grandsons, brothers, uncles, nephews. Then come the King of the Belgians, the Archbishop of Canterbury, the Lord Chancellor, other Archbishops, Officers of the Court, Dukes, eldest sons of Royal Dukes, Marquises, eldest sons of Dukes, and so on through Earls, Viscounts, Bishops, Barons, Officers of the Royal Household, Knights of the Garter, Privy Councillors, Lord Chief Justice and other Judges, Baronets, Bannerets, Knights, Esquires, Clergymen, Barristers, Physicians, Officers of Army and Navy, Citizens, Burgesses. Women follow in the same order, except as noted above.

In society, and on all but state occasions, all these nice distinctions are laid aside. Honour is paid to age, merit, genius, beauty, accomplishments, and whatever can or ought to command our respect, esteem, or admiration. The best society is that which is most free from artificial distinctions, and where it is more to be a lady than a duchess; and a simple gentleman, without rank or fortune, can, by the mere force of talents and manners, stand in the highest place. It is only at formal dinner parties that any trouble is made about precedence, and then only in the order of going to the dining-room and sitting at table.

In the street, the place nearest the wall is the place of honour, because of safety. We give the wall to the aged, to women, to all to whom we wish to defer, I should be sorry to know any gentleman, whatever his rank, who would not turn out and even step off the sidewalk for the poorest woman carrying a baby or any burthen.

In a crowded thoroughfare, the rule is for everyone to keep to the right. In riding and driving in this country, but only here, so far as I know, people turn to the left in meeting; in passing they take the right. Railway trains keep the left side of the track.

A gentleman not offering his arm to a lady on a staircase, usually precedes her going up, and follows her coming down. On a ship, one keeps to the leeward of a superior. The chief officer is the first to step on deck, and the last to leave it.

As a general rule, we do well to conform to the customs of the place or country we are in, showing thereby our friendly respect to the people we are among. If we visit a church, we should behave as nearly as possible like those who worship in it. If we cannot conscientiously do this, we had better keep away. So a republican, visiting a monarchical country, should be careful to pay the customary respect to royalty, and to conform generally to social usages. The first Christian Missionaries to China found their way to the hearts of the people by adopting their dress, learning their code of etiquette, and conforming, as far as possible, to their customs.

The way to learn all one needs to know of the etiquette and manners of any society is to be quiet, self-possessed, and observant. Notice what well-bred and easy-mannered persons do, and follow their example. Never be ashamed of not knowing anything, but take the first opportunity to ask someone what you wish to know and cannot find out for yourself. A request for information is always flattering. Everyone is naturally pleased to show his superiority. Everyone is happy to give information to another, and guide him in the way he should go. People whom I should not like to ask for sixpence, freely give any amount of information, advice, or criticism. The very young man who wishes to improve his manners, will do well to put himself under the tuition of some lady older, perhaps considerably older, than himself, who, if he is docile, sensible, and grateful, will be delighted to teach him all he needs to know.

CONVERSATION

'Good talk' says the author of *Realmah*, 'is ever one of the choicest things in the world, and wins all people who come within its sphere.' Our social life is chiefly conversation – a turning together – the interchange of thought and feeling.

It is probable that all animals which associate with each other have language and conversation – some method of communicating information and expressing feeling. Ants and bees evidently talk with each other. When a prize is at hand, or danger threatens, the whole swarm is quickly told of it. They act in concert. They carry on complicated operations quite impossible without some power of conversation. The hen clucking to her brood calls them to the food she has discovered, gathers them under her wings, or gives warning of danger when she sees a hawk hovering in the sky. In a morning of spring, when the groves are full of melody, it must be that the melody has meaning, and that every phrase is understood, at least by birds of the same species. The lowing and bleating herds must also talk to each other. Dogs talk together, and they learn to understand us much better than we do them. The elephant has a very human comprehension of the orders of his keeper; and elephants who live in societies hold converse with each other.

'Steed threatens steed in high and boastful neighings.' The conversation of animals is natural or instinctive. If men ever had such a natural language, it has been lost. Instead of it we have hundreds of dialects made up of artificial, conventional, articulate sounds. What we have of instinctive language consists in gestures, grimaces, tones, modulations, inflexions, emphasis. Whatever language men speak, we know by sight and hearing whether they are pleased or vexed – whether they hate or love.

Our conversation is therefore partly natural or instinctive in tones, gestures, and expressions of the countenance, laughter, tears, and all the picturesqueness and melody of speech; and partly artificial and conventional in the use of words, or articulate sounds, whose meaning has been agreed upon. The beauty of all conversation consists in the choice and admixture of these two elements of language. We like to see those with whom we converse. The glances of the eye, the flushings of the cheek, the smiles or frowns, and all expressions of feeling on the mobile face, the motions of the head, the slight shrugs of the shoulders tell as much as, often far more than, the spoken words. Then how much more expressive is speech than writing. The written word has one meaning – the spoken word may have a dozen. We vary it with every mode of utterance. Written language, however carefully taken down, may give but the faintest idea of the eloquence, or even the meaning of a speaker. Thus no reporter can do justice to some orators, who have produced the strongest impression upon multitudes of hearers; and people delight us with the warmth, grace, and vivacity of their conversation, whose words, if accurately written down, would seem tame and insipid. The life that goes with the speech is wanting. In reading, words have what we are able to put into them. Good readers are those who can express the sense and sentiment of a writer as he would wish to express them himself in speech.

As we all talk more or less; as conversation is the life, the nervous circulation of the social body, we should try to talk well. To do this we must have intelligence, knowledge, facts of interest, things and thoughts, ideas and sentiments, which others may wish to hear; and we must be able to convey our ideas in a clear and pleasant manner.

Everyone can bring something to the common stock of conversation – the commerce of knowledge and thought, where all freely receive and freely give. The preacher is paid for his sermons, the lawyer for his opinions, the doctor for his prescriptions, the author for his writings, but conversation is generous and free. It asks only reception and appreciation. Those who have are eager to bestow their treasures, and good listeners are as necessary as good talkers, and required in much larger proportions, for to every talker there ought to be ten listeners. When companies divide into couples, and a large room is full of the hum of private discussions, it can scarcely be called conversation. A large party must break into groups, but not into couples. When people know how to listen as well as how to talk, the larger the group the more life and variety to the conversation. I doubt if two persons can properly occupy themselves in conversation without an apology to the rest of the company.

It is well that every group should have its leader or centre; not always the one who talks most or best, but the one who listens, manages, suggests, and draws out or gives opportunities to others. A lady of tact and intelligence does this best. She guides conversation as the coxswain steers the boat, or the four-in-hand driver manages his team, checking the restive, touching up the dull, and keeping all in order and up to their work. A lady who can do this, not only for a single group, but for a drawing room full of guests, arranging compatibilities, and seeing that all are having the best enjoyment of their opportunities, is fit to be a hostess and social queen.

If the first qualification for conversation is to know now to speak, it is, in some ways, a more important one to know how to listen. We draw out, encourage, excite, and elevate by our manner of receiving and accepting what one says. The orator gets life, suggestion, and support from his audience. He is borne up by the waves of their appreciation. The supply follows the demand. Good listeners make good talkers.

A good listener never interrupts, unless very adroitly with a question or objection, which is also a suggestion and help to the speaker. A good listener is patient and courteous, and does his best to give everyone his full opportunity. He does not necessarily agree with what is said. The free expression of differences of opinion is the life of conversation; but a courteous, and even friendly toleration is its necessity. There is a limit to the proper expression of feeling in conversation; and dissent may be very decided, without being violent or disrespectful.

We must have the same regard to the rights of others in conversation that we ought to have in business. Let every fact have its place, and every argument its weight. To interrupt, overbear, crush with clamour, silence with assumption, are violations of equity, as well as politeness. We may discuss freely, but never dispute; we may fairly controvert, but we have no right to denounce. And we can never impute bad motives to persons who hold opinions contrary to our own. A man may be wrong in his facts, absurd in his logic, and his doctrines may be ever so distasteful, or even dangerous, but he must be treated with kindness and civility, and his motives judged of with charity.

It is better, perhaps, that subjects which excite strong emotions, and are liable to produce partisan conflicts, should not be made subjects of conversation in general society. In a country where there are so many religious sects and opinions, giving rise to violent animosities, it may be well to banish religious discussions entirely; but when newspapers, pamphlets, books, treating of such subjects, are read by almost every one, it is very difficult to keep them out of general conversation; and conversation is, as it must be, more polite than writing. Men write of Roman Catholics, or Ritualists, for example, what they would never think of saying to them at a dinner-table. At a table where Brigham Young was a guest, no one would abuse the Mormons. The strongest Churchman would be civil to Mr Spurgeon; and Mr Spurgeon, I have no doubt, would treat His Holiness the Pope with all the courtesy due to his character and position. Thus society is a civiliser, and men of the most opposite views learn to treat each other like gentlemen.

To be a good listener, then, we must be very tolerant – not of error itself, but of its expression; not to the fault, but of the individual who is faulty. As one may detest the sin, and yet love the sinner, so one may reprobate what he esteems a false opinion with entire calmness and unfailing courtesy. To be a good listener, we must be entirely self-possessed, 'swift to hear, slow to speak, slow to wrath.' It is polite to listen; it is often a real charity. We gain more esteem by what we hear than by what we say. Perhaps the highest art in conversation is to make others talk. The man who hears you may be bored; the man who talks to you never is. He may be dissatisfied with your views; he is sure to be pleased with his own. And if a man is tiresome, or becomes so by talking too much, the best way to escape is by a compliment. Thank him for the pleasure he has given, and do not deprive others of the benefit of listening to his instructive remarks. We are not to be insincere; for everybody is instructive, though too much of some kinds of instruction may become monotonous. But a man of tact will be able at any time to give a new turn to conversation, and adroitly throw it into the hands of a more entertaining coloquist.

Everyone who goes into society – that is, who meets his fellowmen anywhere where conversation is possible, should know how to talk. I have written of speech as an accomplishment. We should speak loud enough to be heard, but not loud enough to stun those who are near us.

Boisterousness is a sort of insolence. But we should speak with perfect distinctness, so as never to be obliged to repeat a sentence. An even flow of speech is a great comfort to the hearers. It is a pain to listen to people who speak painfully, and find it difficult to get out their words. Speech should be easy, simple, graceful, and, if possible, picturesque, animated, and melodious. There is no music like beautiful speech.

But the matter of speech must be as choice as the manner is good. When we have said good morning, and made our congratulations or condolences on the state of the weather, and enquired about the health and conditions of mutual acquaintances, there is still something to be said. The world is full of interesting things, near or remote. Generally the near things are the most interesting. A burglary in the same street is more to us than the destruction of a city in another hemisphere.

We cannot compel people to take an interest in the things that we consider most important. We must take the topics that are current at the time. If a great war is raging, it absorbs all interest. So a trial at law may fill newspapers and conversation. Some political movement, or some social scandal may be the topic of the time. We must do our best with the materials at hand; and what we need is a point of departure. When the conversation is begun, no one can quite tell what course it will take.

In talk there must be no monopoly. No one person ought ever to speak more than two or three minutes. Anecdotes or stories can only be used for illustration, and the most interesting one should not last five minutes. Give lectures, or go to lectures if you will, but there must be no lectures in conversation. Every person who wishes to speak must have the opportunity to do so just as much as to eat and drink; and when a man has had his say on any subject, he cannot do better than to turn to some silent, but interested person – one of another sex if convenient, and see what new contribution can be made to the common stock.

And almost every conversation is the better if seasoned with wit and enlivened with gaiety. Humour is a gift, like poetry or music. Fun bursts out like fire. Wit is different. Some are quick-witted, and are always ready with some pertinent or impertinent remark, but others think out their retorts, as Byron did, and only come to them next day. Such people do well to think over all probable matters of conversation, and have their impromptus ready. But why should not a man who is giving a party have his good things laid out with his clean linen, and all his jokes, and puns, and repartees in readiness, as one packs a hamper for a picnic?

With a full mind and a good memory, no one can be at fault. The good memory supposes order and self-possession. But all conversation should seem to be spontaneous, and prompted by the occasion. Story-tellers should have good memories, not only for the details of their anecdotes, but to avoid telling them too often in the same company. The same story should not be told more than twice, unless urgently demanded.

The specially social quality is good nature, amiability, the desire to please, the kindness of heart that avoids giving offence, and cannot bear to hurt any one's feelings. A good-natured person may frankly disagree with you, but he never offends. He quarrels good-naturedly. He boxes with gloves on – when he fences ever so deftly, there is a great soft button on the end of his foil. He may satirise, ridicule, open up all your weaknesses and absurdities, but so kindly that you cannot help loving him. He cannot say a harsh, hard, bitter, or contemptuous thing, because he has no hardness and no contempt. This is simple, natural goodness, like the goodness of fond and friendly animals. It may not be a high moral virtue; there is no particular merit in it any more than in beauty or any natural gift, but it is a very delightful quality, and those who do not possess it should imitate those who do. Just as we avoid in person, dress, or manners, anything that may give disgust or pain, so must we do in our conversation. We must no more use vulgar expressions than we would wear vulgar garments. Our talk should be as clean as our fingers. We should no more bite one with our words than with our teeth.

An angry word is as bad as a blow, and a satirical word is like a sting. If we are never to say anything to a person which will give him disgust or pain, we must be even more careful not to say anything of any one which will injure him in the estimation of others. Playful, good-natured criticism upon the little foibles and peculiarities of others, may be no harm, and even useful, but it ceases to be good-natured when it gives pain. Slander is a sin much worse than theft. Charity forbids that we should even tell the truth, when that truth can wound and injure. The best rule is to say all the good we can of every one, and to refrain from ever saying evil, unless it becomes a clear matter of duty to warn someone against him.

At table, every subject must be such as will not interfere with appetite and digestion. The conversation should be light, so as not to tax the brain when the life-forces are gathered to the stomach. It should be cheerful, which is another name for convivial. It is better not to talk of food, because if people speak of their likings, they may also speak of their dislikes, and what one is fond of may disgust another. There should never be mentioned at table any subject of possible disgust. Some say one should never mention at table anything which might not properly be placed upon it. Consequently one should never mention disease, or medicine, or anything connected with either. If one speaks of a voyage, he must omit the interesting fact of his having been sea-sick.

At all well-regulated water-cure establishments there is an absolute rule against the mention of disease or treatment. There may be no harm in saying, 'I had a glorious douche this morning', but the discussion that might arise is to be avoided. Generally, nothing must ever be said at table which could, directly or indirectly, excite disgust. No more must there be said anything to excite anger. This is, of course, the rule in all conversation; but it is especially dangerous to get angry over one's dinner. Perfect good nature, and a certain degree of hilarity, befit every feast. People who are serious and thoughtful at table, are liable to become dyspeptics. The conversation should therefore be easy, playful, and mirthful. Party politics and sectarian religion may therefore as well be postponed. Speeches at dinners are a mistake. A man who is going to make a long set speech cannot properly dine.

Men who have just dined are not in a condition to listen to serious speeches. If speeches are made, they should be well besprinkled with 'roars of laughter'.

In England, ladies leave the table soon after the dessert is served, and the gentlemen draw closer for wine and talk. A few years ago they drank much more wine than was good for them, and much of their conversation was quite unfit for ladies to hear. In our better days, no gentleman dares to reel back to the drawing-room; and the conversation of gentlemen is never indecent. Under these reformed conditions, why should the ladies leave the table at all, until all can go together as they came? There is no reason, but that Englishmen cling to all the old customs, however unreasonable. If a thing has been done once, the precedent is established, and it must be done forever. But nothing can be done the first time, because it is unprecedented. In France, ladies and gentlemen leave the table together. We have books of the table talk of famous talkers from Martin Luther – much of whose talk, even that printed, not many ladies would like to read – to Sidney Smith, one of the most genial and benevolent, as well as wittiest of coloquists; still, the dinner-table is not the place for intellectual conversation. The tea-table suits it better. The reception and the *conveszatione*, where the refreshment of the body is quite a secondary matter, are places for real conversation. Morning parties on the hills, in forests, on shaded lawns, where well-assorted groups can read and talk, are perhaps best of all.

To talk well, we must have both sense and knowledge; but one who has sense must have knowledge also. The experience and observation of every one's life is an education. He who knows himself knows the most of what is worth knowing; and all knowledge consists in self-knowledge, and the knowledge of our relations to the world around us. Common sense, or the sense of things common to human beings, our thoughts and feelings, and the matter of our lives, is the best sense we can have, and what helps us most in conversation.

We do not usually talk about the sciences. How seldom are geology or astronomy mentioned in conversation. Chemistry is less discussed than cookery. Men do not talk much of geography or geometry. History and biography come nearer to us, and still nearer politics and commerce, literature and art – that is, the newest novels, and poems and pictures, or the songs of the season, are conversational there is egotism and a temptation to some sort topics in the best society. One must read the current literature, and know what is going on in the world; but the best of all knowledge for conversation is the knowledge of men, women, and life.

And of all talents none is so useful as sympathy. When we feel with and for our fellows, and can enter into the thoughts and feelings of every one we meet, rejoicing in their joys, sharing in their sorrows, ready with comfort and help, then our conversation is a delight. We win all hearts by sympathy more than by all gifts and accomplishments. The sympathetic attract; the cold and heartless repel. We admire beauty, elegance, wit, eloquence: but we love geniality, friendliness, goodness.

It is not necessary that these qualities should be expressed in words. Professions of benevolence, or of any virtue, are repulsive. All egotism is selfishness, and selfishness is the quality directly opposed to benevolence. We can show our love of virtue by practising it, and recognising and praising it in others. Our sympathy comes out in a thousand ways, and it is seen and felt by those who need it. It beams in the face of a kind-hearted man or woman, and reveals itself in the tones of the voice, and every mode of expression. Sympathy especially shows itself in the power of adapting ourselves to others – of becoming all things to all men, that we may do them good.

There are some faults we must carefully avoid in conversation; faults of character, and faults of manner. It is not only our right, but it is our duty to conceal our faults. If we have bad feelings we must suppress the expression of them. If I am angry, must I vent my rage? So if I feel emotions of pride or vanity, am I to strengthen them by giving them expression in words or actions? Certainly not. Everyone in the company of others is on his good behaviour. People who snap and snarl at home are polite enough abroad; and the more they are under such restraint the better. Society civilises. The more we bring people together the more we improve their manners; manners become habits; habits mould hearts.

The man who boasts becomes ridiculous. Modesty is a virtue highly appreciated by everybody's self-esteem. If I vaunt myself, my family, my property, my deeds, and make myself or any of my belongings the subject of conversation, I offend more or less all who listen to me. It is distasteful to the meek, and offensive to the haughty. It is only in droll, bantering ways that people can speak of themselves, and the less they do so in any way the better. A man may, of course, tell his own story, simply and frankly, without consciousness of merit or affectation of modesty. He may relate things of himself very much to his credit, if there is no vain glorying.

'Of their own merits modest men are dumb.' A man can talk best of what he knows most about, but of vain glory when a man speaks much of his own profession or employment. We must talk of what interests others rather than ourselves; and in any case consult the tastes and enjoyments of others – the greatest good of the greatest number. There is a proverbial prohibition against 'talking shop'. The clergyman is not to wear his surplice in the drawing-room, nor the lawyer his wig. The doctor who has spent the morning in consultations should be glad to rest from patients and diseases. Society is for recreation; so everyone can leave his work, and give play to faculties which need exercise. Still, when questions arise in conversation it is natural to appeal to those who have special knowledge.

It is best in all conversation to avoid technicalities not generally understood. As we modulate our voices so as to reach the most distant person in the group, so we should adapt our language to the comprehension of the most ignorant. The skilful orator is careful not to speak over the heads of his hearers when he wishes to convince, and reserves any high flight for the corruscations of his peroration. In conversation such displays are out of place. We talk to instruct and amuse; and amusement should be the vehicle of instruction.

Slang. Doubtless it cannot be entirely banished; but it should be used very sparingly, and only the newest and best. Very nice slang becomes incorporated into the language. Poor slang has its day, and is thrown aside like last year's fashions. Most slang quickly becomes vulgar. One day some clever or fashionable person, economical of breath, said 'thanks' instead of 'I thank you.' Many followed his example, but when the shop-boys began to pelt him with 'thanks'; he returned at once to the more elaborate expression. There was a time when the most opposite things were 'awfully jolly', but the alarming phrase went out with crinoline or chignons. There is a slang dictionary which it might be well to look over so as to see what to avoid.

Pet phrases and hackneyed common-places of expression destroy originality. The talk of many persons is entirely made up of these threadbare formularies. Many sermons are a patchwork of them; and we hear speeches of men of celebrity which consist almost entirely of conventional phrases. All this we should carefully avoid. Life is too short to spend in that way. The man who must talk twenty minutes when he has really nothing, or next to nothing, to say may be excused for padding out with a mess of verbiage. But in conversation the more we condense, the quicker we hit the nail on the head, the better. Diffuseness bores. A dozen persons are eager to express an opinion, or launch a witticism, and you pointlessly prose away for fifteen minutes. Only persons of very high position can be tiresome with impunity.

The stage gives us models for conversation. There are no long speeches or stories. No dramatist dares make an actor speak uninterruptedly for five minutes. Even the set orations in Shakespeare are delightfully short and to the purpose. No audience will hear a long, dull story badly told. Everywhere there must be fire, spirit, animation, deep earnestness, or lively fun, something to interest or amuse, to excite our sympathy or provoke our mirth. A social party is an improvised comedy in which every actor should play his part as well, at least, as if he were on the stage with pay and plaudits. The actor, it is true, has his part written for him, studies it carefully and practices with frequent rehearsals; but in our social life each has his part, with all his lifetime to make it perfect; with constant rehearsal, and daily improvement in thought, expression, and action. Surely this work in earnest is better than any make-believe.

What we need for the conversation of social life is a good heart, a full mind, an earnest desire to please, the tact and delicacy never to offend, the motives of a Christian, and the manners of a gentleman.

If you have read much and remember what you have read; if you have travelled much, and can describe well what you have seen and heard; if you have seen much of the world, and possess a fund of observation and anecdote; or if you are simply a clear thinker, and can easily arrange your thoughts, and group them into a picturesque expression, you have a right to a large share of the conversation of any circle.

Let your words be as fit and well chosen as your clothes. Avoid coarseness and vulgarity in speech, as you would in costume. Dress your best thoughts, in words and phrases of corresponding beauty. Plain and homely subjects do not bear finery of expression; but a delicate sentiment may well be embellished with the flowers of rhetoric.

The first salutation may decide your fate with respect to the person you salute. Boldness may disgust, bashfulness seem a confession of meanness. People are inclined to take you at your own estimate or price, unless you appear to set it too high, when they are put on their guard not to be cheated.

Let your first address, then, be firm, quiet, dignified, cordial, but not too forward; confident, but not presuming, and as easy, natural, and unaffected, in air, gesture, and language, as possible. There are people with whom you are acquainted and at your ease in two minutes. But such persons are entirely at ease with themselves; entirely natural in their expression of themselves. They are what they seem, and seem what they are.

The common principles of equity or justice preside over conversation. All principles are universal in their application. We have no more right to be intrusive, or despotic, or overbearing, or in any way dishonest in our conversation, than in any other mode of action. We have no more right to pass off a counterfeit sentiment or a false opinion, than we have a counterfeit note or a false coin.

Conversation should, therefore, first of all, be honest. There is a certain allowance for irony, raillery, satire, and jocularity, as there is for games, sports, and pastimes; but whatever purports to be an expression of fact, or opinion, or feeling, should be altogether truthful.

Two things we must never do. We must never tell a falsehood, and never accuse another of telling one. The one is a great wrong, the other a great insult. A lie is in the intent to deceive, and thereby injure. The untruth of badinage and drollery has no bad motive, and neither deceives nor injures. A mystification is not meant to harm anyone. Irony may be the opposite of literal truth. But real, essential truthfulness is the first element of social confidence; and we should be carefully accurate in all serious speech, and never accuse another of what we would not do ourselves. If we doubt the correctness of a statement, we must express that doubt with delicacy and politeness.

Profanity is no longer admissible. Gentlemen do not curse and swear as they did, such gentlemen as there were, in the last generation. It has gone out with drunkenness. No subject or expression should ever be introduced in conversation which can shock a pious mind. Reverence is an element of true manliness. Even when we may think some belief absurd or some devotion superstitious, we are not to hurt the feelings of those who hold the belief or practice the devotion. We must do as we would be done by in these matters, and respect all conscientious convictions.

It has been said that the hardest thing to tolerate is intolerance. But intolerance is bad manners, and bad manners are intolerable. The rule is not to intrude our own beliefs or unbeliefs, and especially the latter, for the assertion of unbelief is an attack upon belief. Infidelity is negation – contradiction. We may excuse the earnestness of one who wishes us to accept his belief, but why should a man wish to convert us to his unbelief? In any case, a man of delicacy and humanity will avoid giving pain.

Indecency of language is banished from all decent society. Equivocal expressions, double entendre, jests which mingle blushes with laughter are no longer tolerated. The novels that were once fashionable have become unreadable – the comedies that once drew crowded and applauding audiences are scarcely read in the closet; the songs and stories that once set the table in a roar are never heard. At the same time, there is less squeamishness and more freedom in the serious discussion of important though disagreeable subjects than formerly. The facts of our social condition cannot be utterly ignored, and earnest discussion must accompany earnest work. The evils of society must be known, that they may be remedied. They must be grappled with, or they cannot be removed. Such matters, however, can be introduced only by common consent, and in accordance with the law of supply and demand. The few should not force their favourite topics upon the many, and the many should have some regard for the feelings and even the prejudices of the smallest minority.

In conversation, questioning is often disagreeable and even offensive. Curiosity may become intrusive. No one likes to be cross-examined. No one likes prying into his private affairs. English people do not like to be questioned about their ages, business, property, or personal relations. There are pertinent and impertinent questions; questions which draw people out, and help them to talk well; but there are also questions which embarrass and annoy. As a rule, it is better to make observations and suggestions than to ask direct questions.

To make a butt of any person in company, to expose him to ridicule, or turn the laughter of the company against him, is as much an outrage as it would be to pull his nose, slap his face, or box his ears. Ridicule is only justifiable where it is a fair game that two can play at; a contest of well-matched wits, who encounter like a couple of wrestlers or fencers.

Men of great genius and varied talent are sometimes almost entirely lacking in conversational powers. Brilliant writers are often very poor talkers – shy, dull, silent, with no power of expression. On the other hand, an extreme volubility of small talk and common-places may accompany the utmost shallowness of mind. There is a power in conversation, as in all modes of expression, which may be termed magnetic. Certain persons impress us deeply with a few simple words, or a quiet gesture, or a mere look. The words are nothing, the action is but a slight and simple movement, yet there is a power in them to charm, to thrill, to subdue us. It is the force of the spirit, the magnetism of a strong and penetrative or sympathetic soul. The same words from another person would not affect us.

This power in an orator or an actor is quite distinct from his subject or his words. It is his own power. He may be speaking on any subject; preaching any doctrine. It is believed by some that this mysterious power is communicated to the manuscripts of certain writers, and even to their printed works.

Inattention, or the appearance of inattention to a person speaking to you, is very bad manners. You should not only listen, but should seem to do so; and do nothing which can detract from that appearance. You need not continually reply, 'yes', 'ah!' 'no', 'you don't say', 'fancy!' These exclamations have the benevolent intention of showing your interest in the speaker, and encouraging him to proceed, but they are something more than is requisite. Listen with a silent, thoughtful, interested or pleased attention. Look at the person who addresses you. Look him clear in the eye, or at least watch the expression of his countenance. An absent-minded person has no business in company. He had better make his body as absent as his mind.

Many admirable conservationists never argue or dispute. They assert the facts they know or believe to be true; they propound such principles as they entertain; they give opinions or make suggestions. If their facts are doubted or denied, they leave them to be settled by observation, testimony, or competent authority. If their principles are questioned, they may state the science or analogies on which they are based. If their opinions are criticised, they only ask for the same toleration they give to others. Their suggestions and surmises are to be taken for what they are worth.

But many persons are fond of disputation. It is a mental exercise – an exciting game – a kind of cerebral gymnastics. Within the bounds of good breeding, and so conducted as not to give annoyance to others, these discussions may be harmless and even advantageous. But they can rarely be entered upon in general society. Men argue, not to be convinced that they are in the wrong – not always to set others right, but to display their skill, or triumph in a contest. Even in public discussions, where two or more able men are pitted against each other, and the partisans of each combatant assemble to hear them, how few are ever converted from one side to the other!

In most discussions, we contend with prejudices, bigotries, and idiosyncrasies. People born and living neighbours grow up Tories and Liberals, Catholics and Protestants, or Unitarians and Trinitarians. How seldom do all the controversies continually going forward, in private conversations, in the pulpit, and by means of the press, convert a religionist, or even a politician, to an opposite faith? Politeness is truly cosmopolitan. It does not ask where one was born, or what he believes, nor even what he does, so long as it is his own personal affair. It only requires that he be a gentleman; and one true gentleman can do nothing to offend another. A bigot cannot be a gentleman, for he must obtrude his own prejudices, and attack those of others. A certain degree of tolerance for a variety of opinions, manners, and morals, adds to the interest of society, and prevents the necessity of excluding so many subjects that nothing remains to talk about. Doubtless the more there is of freedom and toleration, the more interesting must be the conversation of any circle.

People who wish to please others pay them compliments, praise them, flatter them. Flattery is indiscreet, insincere, or selfish praise. Undeserved praise is the severest censure. Indiscreet praise exposes us to the jealousy of others. Insincere praise is lying with a benevolent or selfish motive. But honest, judicious praise is a matter of justice as well as kindness; and it not only gives pleasure, but is often a real benefit. We are probably too reticent in this respect – too stingy of our applause. It is better to freely, generously, graciously commend whatever we find of excellence, and even all well meant, even if unsuccessful, efforts. What a stimulant to effort is the hearty greeting of an artist on his first appearance before an audience! The enthusiastic applause which rewards success is very delightful. We cannot always give the same expressions of applause in society – but we can and ought to give a frank expression of our good will, pleasure, admiration, and gratitude. We want more simple heartiness in such matters, and much less of that reticence which seems like stupidity, indifference, envy, or contempt.

The rules of politeness are never at variance with the principles of morality. Whatever is really impolite is really immoral. We have no right to offend people with our manners or conversation. We have no right to deal with or be influenced by gossip about the people we meet. Their private affairs are none of our business. If we believe a man to be unfit company for us, we must not invite him, but if we meet him where he has been invited by others, we must treat him with civility. If we know a man or woman to be a grave offender, we cannot use that knowledge to injure him or her, unless it is absolutely needful for the protection of others. The greatest and best men in the world have been assailed with calumny. The purest and noblest do not always escape it. We cannot investigate – as a rule we must disregard – all slanders. Where great offences become notorious, the offenders must be excommunicated. In all other cases we must give everyone the benefit of a doubt; apply charitable constructions, hope for the best, and consider every one innocent until he is proven guilty.

There are little blunders in conversation we do well to avoid. It is better not to call out the names of persons we address. We have no right to call attention to the business or profession of any person, or our own, or to introduce private affairs into general society. Few people like nicknames; and we must give people their proper designations, unless they really wish us to do otherwise. Avoid expletives and exaggerations, and deal sparingly with exclamations. You cannot laugh without explaining what you are laughing at. You cannot whisper without apology. Do not speak to any person in a language a third party cannot understand. This does not, of course, apply to the case of a foreigner, whom you address in his own language – but even then you ought to interpret. Do not quote Latin or Greek in the presence of those who may be presumed to be ignorant of either.

The rules for conversation are the same as for all behaviour – simplicity, modesty, a calm self-possession, reverence for age and superiority of every kind, a tender respect for women, a desire to please others and promote their happiness, a forgetfulness of self, or utter absence of all selfishness, care of the absent; justice, benevolence, charity.

THE FAMILY

The family is the basis or unit of society. 'God hath set the earth in families', families unite in tribes; tribes join for mutual protection, and form nations; but the family is the pivot on which human society revolves. It is the natural grouping of humanity, and the model of all larger associations. Family relations are our first, dearest, and last relations. Family duties are our chief duties in life, and in the family we find our greatest happiness. Other associations and duties are of a more temporary, exceptional, or artificial character. Birth, marriage, life, and death are in the family. It is easy to see, therefore, that our behaviour in the family relations is the most important of all to our happiness.

The English people believe that they have family life in its highest perfection, and that they, of all peoples, know most of the comforts of home. But some English writers of our day have discovered that family life exists also among our nearest Continental neighbours in great purity and affection, and in larger groupings than in England – grandparents, children, and grandchildren living together in large mansions, or clusters of dwellings, in mutual love and help, and forming beautiful societies. In this way aged parents are not deserted and left to end their days in loneliness; brothers and sisters are not separated; there are nephews and nieces as well as children; cousins make a wider companionship for the young, and various families are interwoven in a network of relationship. In England, and still more in America, there is too much separation and isolation of families. The groups are too small. When the husband is engaged in his business, or taking his comfort at a club, his wife is pining in solitude, or driven to dissipation. Family life is too restricted, and wanting in many of its natural advantages and enjoyments.

When, these patriarchal families are broken up by death or inevitable separation, there is no reason why groups of families, drawn together by mutual sympathy, should not be formed. Friends might live together in close relationship – brothers, sisters cousins by adoption; enjoying the economies as well as the pleasures of such association. There would be economies of rent, service, purchase and preparation of food, and of all the cares of housekeeping, by such co-operation. In a large group of persons someone will have a special talent for housekeeping, another for education, another for dress, and so on. The impulse of youth is tempered by the wisdom of age. In such a family society there springs up a devotion to the general good, instead of isolate selfishness, and a corporate industry which promotes the general welfare. Every talent finds employment. There is a larger scope for life – a fine emulation, an orderly ambition. Women would find their sphere and use.

There must be a limit to the expansion of such a family of families. Every social body has its natural proportions. The full hive must swarm. Nations must divide when their affairs become too cumbrous.

The closer the relations of any society the more important become the manners, morals, behaviour of its members. 'How can two walk together unless they be agreed?' One leads and governs; the other follows and obeys. They may alternate – take turns in mastery, each guiding in what he or she knows best – but the principle of order is a necessity for all unity of life. The family must have its head with very despotic authority, however tenderly exercised. The word despot means ruler of a house. In the house itself the mother is usually the despot – the father governs in a wider sphere. The husband is the head of the wife; the wife is the heart of the husband. The supreme motive of each is the happiness of the other – and by happiness I mean here and always, highest or ultimate good. The husband lives for his wife, the father for his children, and the wife and mother holds corresponding relations. The responsibilities of parents to their children are very serious. Every child has a right to health, nurture, education, a training in some useful avocation, and a fair start in life; and no man has the right to beget a child without the reasonable prospect of performing these paternal duties. No woman has the right to marry without a reasonable prospect of provision for a family.

If parents are not healthy, they cannot give health to their children. If they have not some means of gaining a livelihood, how can they give them a support? If they neglect their education, what can they look for but misfortune and disgrace?

We hear of the respect and gratitude which children owe to their parents; but parents have this to earn by respect for the rights of their offspring; and many parents make respect and gratitude impossible. 'Honour thy father and mother', implies reciprocal duties, and the duties of parents come first, and begin before their children are born. Good children are born of good fathers and mothers. They are what their parents make them in their birth and training. Parents and children stand to each other in the relation of cause and effect. It must be in a large degree their own fault if parents are not honoured and loved, at least during the early years of their children. If they want order they must be orderly – if they want love they must be loving.

Where husband and wife love each other, their children will love them. It is their inheritance, and the sad reverse of this is terribly true. There can be no worse misfortune to a child than to be born of parents who do not love each other. Hence, where there is no love there should be no marriage and no family. As the essence of marriage is a mutual love, this is also the true condition of the parental relation.

Parents who really love their children sometimes put on a hard, cold manner toward them, refraining from all expressions of affection, as if it might interfere with their authority. But it is better to govern by love than by fear, and no motive is so strong as the desire to please those we love, and the dread of offending them. The quick and ready obedience of affection is better than any that can be compelled by fear of punishment. The father and mother rule best in the tender love of their children. The sooner the child becomes the trusted friend of the parent, the better for the happiness of both.

But the authority of the parent is still to be exercised, if necessary, for the good of the child. Every child has a right to parental guidance, and, when he needs it, of parental control.

The child who falls ignorantly into any evil against which a parent might have warned him, must blame his parent – and myriads of men and women suffer all their lives for the want of such parental warnings. A child should be taught whatever it needs to know. It should be warned against every peril to its health and life. And who so fit as the parent to save his child from danger? In this matter there is an awful neglect, and consequently an awful wreck of life. God has placed the bodies and souls of children in charge of their parents, and woe is theirs if they neglect their duty.

Parents should see that their children have all the conditions of health – that their bodies are made clean with the daily bath that all children love – that their clothing is clean, porous, comfortable – that they have very simple pure food at regular intervals, and are not excited with gross or high seasoned food, or pampered with dainties. No child should ever taste bacon, and it is better without flesh of any kind. It should have no tea, coffee, chocolate, or even cocoa, and no beer or spirits. No child is the better for one of these things – it is the worse for any of them. The food of childhood is bread, or its equivalents, milk, fruit. The sweetest, most nutritious, and most healthful bread for children, and for everybody, is made from the whole meal of good wheat – unbolted wheat, as it was eaten before sieves and bolting cloths were invented. As the brown bread of the bakers is not always made of honest meal, each family should have a little mill of its own. Coarsely ground wheat made into porridge, and eaten with milk or syrup, is excellent food. Fruit is as healthful as it is delicious to the unperverted tastes of childhood, whose instincts should be respected. Children ought never to be forced to eat what they do not like. The highest authority in diet is a healthy appetite. The more simple and natural the food of children the better for their health and happiness. With cleanliness, good food and good air, every child born with a good constitution must grow up to maturity, with the best prospects of a long and happy life. Give the conditions of health, before birth and after birth, and there is no need to dread the diseases of infancy. Either children will not have them at all, or they will be but purifying processes, free from pain or danger. Health is the natural condition of every vegetable and every animal.

Disease is always an artificial or abnormal condition. It is the first duty of every parent to give the conditions of health to his children; and the next to give them the education, training, and exercise or discipline of life that they require; to restrain them from evil, and gently, affectionately, but still firmly, to guide them in the way in which they should go.

The child should love and honour his parents, as every well-born and well-trained child must and will. It is a natural consequence. Father and mother are the authors of its being – earthly creators; so that God is called our Heavenly Father; and the earthly father and mother are next to Him in our reverence and love. The mother has the closest and tenderest relation. It was her dear body that sheltered and nourished us before and after we were born; and she has the right to our tenderest love and devotion all the days of her life. Surely I need not enlarge upon the duty of son or daughter to the mother that bore them. The voice of nature is the voice of God, saying, 'Honour thy father and mother'.

The obligations of these relations are mutual. Parents have imperative duties toward their children. They must cherish them in infancy, and guide and educate them in youth. No government can do a parent's duty to his child. He is responsible to the state that his child becomes a good citizen. Doing his duty, the parent has a right to love, reverence, obedience in youth, and comfort and support in age. In our strong middle life it is alike our duty to support the tottering steps of infancy and age. Happy are they who have the love of those who have just come into the world, and the blessing of those who are just leaving it. The blessing of the Father of all rests upon those who deserve alike the blessings of their parents and their children.

Brothers and sisters are natural friends and allies in the struggle of life. It is a beautiful and blessed relationship. Everyone feels what children of the same father and mother ought to be to each other – dearest friends, tenderest companions – loving, faithful, helpful, devoted to each other. I have a strong feeling that brothers and sisters should have more enjoyment of this relationship, and more of the advantage of mutual help, and the beneficial influence they can exert upon each other. They are separated too early and too much. They

ought to be more educated together, and to share each other's
employments and amusements. Boys are hurried off to schools
with other boys; girls shut up with girls. Surely nature has not
intended such a separation. The family is the model of the
school and of society; and I believe that the more children
and youths of both sexes are together the better for their
character and manners, and that the result of the reciprocal
influence of the sexes on each other is to make boys more
manly and girls more womanly, than when they are kept apart.
The sweetest friend, the most delightful mentor of a boy is an
elder sister, and who can a girl so love and trust as a chivalric
brother? If it be, as everyone feels, a great loss to have no
brother or no sister, is it not a loss to be deprived of their
society just when it is most needed and can be most enjoyed?
I am sure that the early years of thousands are marred, and
of many blasted, by these unnatural separations – unnatural
and needless. The education of the two sexes should be almost
the same. They need the same sciences, and almost the same
accomplishments. They join in the same recreations. It is not
for the good of either that they should be separated. Family
ties are too valuable, too sacred, to be wantonly broken.

And when children have grown up, and become men and
women, I think they should not hastily separate from their
parents and from each other. Very sad is the desolation of
aged people whose children have left them alone in the world.
Why not group together and strengthen and help each other?
If some must emigrate, why not all go together, and make a
larger home in another hemisphere?

Marriages add to the number of children, and give us new
brothers and sisters. Some protest against the doctrine – but
people really marry all their husband's or wife's relations.
I know few more shameful things in recent literature than
the fun made of mothers-in-law. One has as much right to
make fun of his own mother as of the mother of his wife.
Her relations are his relations. In a certain sense a man may
leave his father and mother and cleave unto his wife; but it
will not be pretended that marriage abrogates the duties of
children to their parents. If we make any difference, we should
be more kind to, and considerate of, our relations by marriage.
The church teaches that we contract a spiritual affinity to the

blood relations of those to whom we are joined in marriage. The laws of England forbid a man to marry his deceased wife's sister. No one thinks of marrying a deceased husband's brother. The father and mother who have children married, should never be allowed to feel that they have lost a son or daughter, but rather that they have gained one; and should feel and be richer and happier for the event.

The property inherited or accumulated by parents is for all their children. Naturally they have all an equal right to it. The law divides equally among daughters; and sons and daughters have equal shares in all property but houses and lands, which go to the eldest son, or his eldest son. The evident intention of this law is, that the possession of all real property shall be a sort of stewardship, and that the land shall be kept together and held by one for the good of all. The eldest son, or heir of an estate, is the representative of the family, the head of the house, the chief of the clan, and it is his duty to attend to the interests of every member. He has no right to use this property selfishly, nor to deprive any one of his natural right of inheritance. He is not only bound to keep the property for his successor, but to administer it for the benefit of the whole family to whom the estate belongs. All property of this kind really belongs to the State, and is held by individuals by various tenures for the general welfare. Great estates were first granted by the Sovereign to the chiefs of tribes, to be administered for the benefit of tenants and labourers, as well as for the landlord and his family. The eldest son or heir to an estate has therefore great responsibilities and duties, taking the place of the father of a family, the chief of a clan, and the administrator of a domain. What is called real estate is not of the nature of private or personal property; but all property, being the result of human labour, brings duties and responsibilities to its possessor. It is only in a limited sense our own. It can be taken, as taxes, for the support of the needy. We have no right to waste or destroy it.

The behaviour of the different members of a family to each other, should correspond with the sacredness of their relationship to each other. Parents should not only be but seem tenderly affectionate to then children. Why conceal the love one feels in every fibre of his heart. The French behave better than the English in this respect. It is beautiful to see French parents with their children, so kind and thoughtful, proud and caressing and they are well repaid.

The fondness of children for their parents must be respectful, and never run into presumption and disobedience. A young man should be more gallantly attentive, more scrupulously polite, to his mother and sisters than to other ladies, and never permit himself to treat any female relative with the familiarity of neglect. The family is the centre of society; and charity, which embraces all humanity, begins at home. Father, son, brother, mother, daughter, sister, owe supreme duties to their nearest relations. In adversity, in affliction, in the deepest misfortunes, the members of a family should be true and faithful to each other. One hears of strange and dreadful things: of men beating their wives; of parents cruelly treating their children; of children ill-treating and neglecting to provide for their parents; of fortunes squandered by the rich and wages spent in drunkenness among the poor; of a daughter turned helpless into the streets because some scoundrel has betrayed her – because she has married against the wishes of her parents; in some cases because she has embraced a religion of which they disapprove. There must have been somewhere cruel stepfathers and stepmothers; but for the honour of humanity, let us hope that all these unnatural perversities are rare, and that the great mass of our fellow-beings respect the sacred ties of family and home.

LOVE

The force with which two atoms, or two masses of matter, tend toward each other, is called attraction, or gravitation. The force with which two human beings are attracted to each other is called love. We have the love of friendship, which exists between persons without distinction of sex; the love of consanguinity between parents and children, brothers and sisters, etc.; the love of the neighbour, nation, race, humanity, philanthropy; and there is the love which draws and binds a man to a woman, and a woman to a man in marriage, and which is the centre and source of all family relations. As the love of the sexes for each other is the means by which the life of the race is maintained upon the earth – by which humanity exists – it is the most important of all human relations; and it is natural that it should very largely fill our thoughts, engage our feelings, enter into our avocations and amusements, and pervade our art and literature. Much of the history and biography of the world, three-fourths of the poetry, and nine-tenths of the fiction, is occupied with this subject. It is the spring of industry, and the chief motive of all human action. It is not possible to exaggerate its importance.

Through the whole domain of animate nature we have the same force in action. The seed of a plant is produced by a wonderful combination of pollen cell and germ cell, male and female elements. We can see them in all our common flowers, stamens and pistils attracted to each other by some mysterious impulse, to fulfil the universal law – increase and multiply. Animals manifest in several ways, according to their instincts, the same attraction of the sexes, and so all life is continued and increased. No subject relating to man and the earth is so interesting as this of the life of the human race and of all races, and no subject is so much neglected. The idea has in some way come to people that botany, natural history, and the most important branches of human physiology, are improper sciences, and that children should grow up, and men and women remain, in all possible ignorance of the means by which they come into existence, and the influences which form and govern their bodies and minds, and produce health or disease, virtue or vice, happiness or misery. I have treated very freely and very fully on these matters, in such a way as I think their importance merits, in *Human Physiology, the Basis of Sanitary and Social Science*, and also in *Esoteric Anthropology* here I can only speak of love, or the attraction of the sexes, in its social aspects and relations, as it guides and influences the behaviour of men and women to each other.

The sentiment of the love of sex shows itself very early in life. Boys and girls are attracted to each other, or shy of each other, which is only a reverse action of the same feeling. A boy is more tender and considerate of girls than of boys. He has for them a feeling of deference, gallantry, chivalry; he is tender, devoted, protective, and feels himself drawn to them, or to some one of them, by an undefinable and irresistible charm. The boy of nine or ten is, in some cases, a romantic and passionate lover, generally of some young lady older than himself, and this first love of boyhood often has an admirable influence upon the character. Little girls are perhaps even more tender and romantic, and in a similar fashion. These early sentiments are not to be ridiculed, but to be made useful. We should treat those who love us in this way with great tenderness and consideration, and use our influence for their improvement and happiness. What will not even these young lovers do for those they love? The sentiment becomes modified as time goes on, changing into a reverent friendship which ought to last through life.

Over a large part of the world love is sacrificed to marriage. Where marriages are arranged by parents, or are made for considerations of property, family, or politics, love is a secondary matter. It may follow marriage; it generally does. Men and women must love, and they commonly love those who are nearest to them, and so fulfil the contract which they have made. But this is a derangement of the natural order of things.

Love is the attraction which draws persons of opposite sexes to each other, and marriage is the natural result of that attraction. This is our ideal of a true life, as may be seen in thousands of romances. To marry two persons who have no acquaintance with, and no attraction for each other, because their positions and fortunes are suitable, and their parents and friends think it a good match, may not work badly in a multitude of instances. The choice may be in many cases better than the parties would have made for themselves – there may not be more unhappiness in such marriages than in an equal number where the parties were free to choose; still, every man and every woman would wish to have full opportunity and free choice in this most intimate and momentous affair of matrimony, feeling that it is safer and more natural to marry those they love, than to take the chance of loving those they marry.

It must, however, be said that love, being a sentiment and a passion, ought to be under the control of reason and conscience. It is instinctive, springing up without our wish, prevailing against our will, stronger than our efforts to repress or control it; but though the attraction cannot always be cast off, it may generally be concealed. A man of pride or principle does not yield to his attraction toward a disreputable woman. In most cases the fact that a person loves another, is sufficient either to paralyse the love we feel, or to greatly modify its character. The general law appears to be that if love is not mutual it soon dies. We do not go on loving those who give us no return. As all true love tends to union for life, it cannot exist where such union is impossible. It must be fed at least by some hope or some imagination. As a rule, those who cannot marry cease to love. Whatever absolutely prevents marriage – whatever motive, of prudence, or pride, or conscience – is a bar to union, generally destroys, in time, the sentiment which can find its only satisfaction in such union.

Happily, the greater number of persons are too prudent to begin to love out of the range of matrimonial possibilities. Young women especially, though they may aspire to those above them, seldom allow their affections to centre on those who are below them in social position. They have instinctive foresight of marriage and maternity. Women look for protection, guidance, help, support in life, and do not readily accept the advances of those who have not the character and qualities which give a reasonable promise of future happiness. This instinct, so strongly manifested among animals, tends in man to the improvement of the race. Men are attracted by beauty and amiability, women by manly vigour and intellectual power. The natural result is the progressive increase in the race of its finest and noblest qualities.

As the natural result of love between the sexes is marriage, it is evident that no love should be permitted to exist in either sex which may not properly come to that consummation. We find, therefore, that passionate love is very rare between near relations. The tendency is to look outward, and strangers are proverbially more attractive than intimate acquaintances. Public opinion, religion, law, and an instinct underlying all, prevent the disorders and misfortunes that would arise from near relations falling in love with each other. They are bound together by other ties; and even friendship is unfavourable to love.

If the proper end of passionate love is marriage, it is evident that there should be but one such love. It is absurd to think of loving two or more persons in a society that permits us to marry but one at a time. As there are almost exactly as many men as women in the world, it is an evident injustice for any man to have several wives, or any woman several husbands. There are just enough men to give every woman a husband, just enough women for every man to have one wife and no more. Monogamy is, therefore, the evident law of nature, and marriage the equal right of all who are fitted for that condition. There being but one marriage, there should be but one love. Marriage is indissoluble, because a man who divorces one woman and marries another, commits the same injustice as he does who marries two at the same time. He has a right only to one wife, the second belongs to another.

Married people who cannot live together may separate, but they have no right to marry again, repeating the process as often as they please. It is an evident, complicated injustice.

It is best, therefore, that everyone approaching the age of love, should clearly understand the object or purpose of love; that it is really a matter of life and death; that love is, in its tendencies and consequences, the most important thing in the natural life; that the welfare and happiness of many generations of human beings may depend upon it; that it may make or mar not only two lives, but a great many lives; that the wise choice of a suitable object of love, and consequently partner in marriage, is really a matter of immeasurable importance.

No man should permit himself to love a woman he cannot marry. If he has the misfortune to become enamoured of such a person, he is bound to hide the secret in his own heart. He has no right to encourage her to love him, or prevent her from loving someone whom she can marry. A man, being married, has no right to make love to any woman but his wife. A married woman can of course have no right to accept the love of any but her husband. The simple rule in all these cases, is for each person to put himself or herself in the place of the other, and do as one would be done by. How would you like it? Let every heart honestly answer that question, and there would be no need of argument. If every man would do as he would be done by, the will of God would be done on earth as it is in heaven.

When the love of a woman springs up in the heart of a man, he should consider first of all whether he has a right to cherish it. Is she one he can marry?

Will she be a help meet for him? Can he proudly take her by the hand in the face of the world, and say, this is the woman I choose above all others to be my wife? Can he look forward to a long life in her company, with business, family, and society? Can they be one in their faith and life? It is rather a serious matter. If two persons are not in a similar social position it is difficult, and when there are incompatible and decided religious convictions, it is still more so. A Catholic cannot marry a Protestant unless the latter agree that all the children shall be educated Catholics. How can a Trinitarian marry a Unitarian? It can be only when each expects to convert the other to his own faith. Where there are insuperable obstacles to marriage, a man cannot honourably make love. He must conquer it as he can, and he has no right to let it be known to its object. On the other hand, if he can look forward to marriage, he has to consider whether he can win the love that seems to him the most desirable thing on earth. The natural way to do this is to manifest his preference by seeking the society of the beloved; and by those delicate attentions naturally prompted by his affection. Every woman knows instinctively or intuitively when she is loved, and she accepts or rejects in her heart. Coquetry may induce her to conceal her own sentiments for a time, that she may secretly watch and enjoy the love she has inspired? Or she may wish to consider all that depends upon her choice; but an honest good girl does not keep her lover long in suspense. She turns to him or from him; or she soon shows him, perhaps, that she wishes to be his friend, and does not wish to be his wife.

It is the custom for a man to ask the father or guardian of the lady of his choice for permission to pay his addresses; but this is a formality. A man does not ask leave unless he thinks he is already accepted by the lady; and she should not give such sign of acceptance unless she feels sure of the approval of her parents, or means to do without it. On the other hand, a man who is paying special attentions to a young lady is sometimes asked what his intentions are, by her relations, who wish to know whether they are honourable – that is, matrimonial. Rather a needless enquiry. If dishonourable, he deserves to be kicked out of the house. No man has the right to dangle about a girl, occupying her time, interesting her feelings, keeping away others, just for his amusement. No man of honour or of decent principle can do so. A male flirt is detestable for his dishonesty and his cruelty. A man cannot be too careful in his behaviour to every woman – careful not to disgust, offend, or hurt in any way – but above all, careful of her affections. Men should be polite, kind, friendly, gallant, protective to all women; being always frank and open in their motives and conduct. Deception, fraud, falsehood are always bad, but they are utterly bad in the conduct of men and women to each other in the affairs of love. So much is at stake that there should be entire honesty between them. An honest woman will not allow a man to deceive himself; and a man should be more careful of a woman, whose position is more delicate, whose reputation is more important, whose heart is generally more susceptible to both affection and suffering. Men have many resources in business and ambition which are denied to women. Even if they have, as some think, as great a capacity as women for the pains of disappointed love, they have stronger and more varied distractions.

Long or short courtships? Circumstances in each case must decide this question. It would be better not to get in love until one is nearly ready to marry – but when the one being in the world who can satisfy us is seen, she must at all hazards be secured. And if two persons are joined in a mutual love, they can easily wait, strong in the support of such mutual affection. The best age for a man to marry is from twenty-five to thirty-five; for a woman from twenty to thirty. Having the needful maturity of age and constitution, they may marry when they have a reasonable prospect of a living, and of being able to provide for their children. No man wishes to ask a woman to take a position of less comfort than she has been accustomed to and has a right to expect; no woman wishes to be a burthen to the man she loves; and no man or woman should wish to become a parent without being prepared to fulfil all the responsibilities of the parental relation.

In all this question of the relation of the sexes – in love and its object and consequences, the children are to be considered. They are the object of love and the motive of marriage. In no case must the sacred rights of a child be violated. There must be marriage, because every child has a right to honourable birth and full parental care. The marriage must be indissoluble, because no child can justly be deprived of either parent, and no parent justly separated from a child. Children are the objects of marriage, marriage is the object of love; love, therefore, must always be subject to the necessities and proprieties of the parental relation. All pure and high love is unselfish, seeking the good and happiness of the object beloved. In a true love, each seeks the other's good, and both join in devotion to the welfare and happiness of their children.

Nature and religion are here at one. The laws of virtue, morality, purity are the same for men as for women. Their rights are the same, their duties are reciprocal. What is wrong for one is wrong for the other. A man has no right to require in his wife what he does not himself practice. Women may have stronger motives to virtuous, conduct than men, but the same principles should govern both; and a man has no more right to have an immoral relation to another woman, than the woman he loves, or to whom he is married, has to have such relation to another man. The injustice done, the injury inflicted, the rights violated, the sin committed, are precisely the same. The law which says 'Thou shalt not commit adultery', makes no exceptions and no distinctions. The jealousy and sense of outrage are as strong in one sex as in the other. A man should be as true and loyal to his wife that is to be as to his wife that is; loyal to the wife he has not yet loved or even seen, but whom he is to see and love, as he wishes the yet unknown mistress and wife to be true and loyal to him. This is the law of nature and the law of God; and though passion may dispute it, no sophistry can set it aside.

Men and women should be very frank with each other. When they love each other with a true unselfish love, there is no benefit in concealing the fact from each other, or from the world. If they are to be married, the sooner they are engaged the better. They enter upon a new position in life, and should feel and enjoy its dignity. They are out of the lists, and stand no longer in the way of others. Each prepares for the coming event. This may be almost the happiest period of one's life; and one might almost wish to prolong this calm security of anticipation.

I might say much more of love, but is it not written in a thousand volumes, and in the hearts of millions? 'The all of life is love', the author of *Realmah* says,

> The test of loving is, that being with the loved person all talk is needless, and that the silence, which is embarrassing sometimes in the presence of the nearest friends and the dearestrelations, is perfect ease, and harmony, and comfort in the presence of the one beloved.

MARRIAGE

A separate chapter on marriage may seem superfluous, after what has been said in the chapters on love and society; but the subject is so large, and the right behaviour of men and women to each other in marriage so important, and the errors now being widely taught are so dangerous, that I must ask the attention of the reader to a few additional paragraphs.

Marriage has been denounced as the grave of love, the slavery of women, legalised prostitution, and by many grievous epithets, for which in the evils, abuses, and miseries of many marriages, there has been only too good foundation. It is true that husbands ill treat their wives, and wives torment their husbands; true that marriage is too often the excuse for the unbridled lust of which wives and children are the victims; but these are not the proper results of marriage, but of the weakness and wickedness, the ignorance and perversity, of man. There is no such disorder in the relations of the sexes in the whole animal creation. Man alone is immoral.

Marriage is the necessity, not of the individual, but of the race. Individuals everywhere remain during their whole lives in celibacy; having no vocation for marriage; having no opportunity; disappointed in not obtaining the wished for partner. For many centuries, hundreds of thousands of men and women have abstained from marriage from motives or religion, solemnly dedicating their lives to the service of God and humanity in perpetual chastity. A much larger number remain unmarried from choice or necessity, without any such high and sustaining motives. In England and other countries, from which there is a large emigration, there is a surplus female population absolutely debarred from marriage. There is no positive obligation to marry, and for many there is no possibility. But men who abstain from marriage, merely that they may live in greater ease and luxury, without the cares and expenses of a family, fail in their social duties, and deprive an equal number of women of their social rights. It is a right of humanity that every man should have a wife who wants one, and every woman a husband; and this, as I have shown, necessitates the monogamic marriage. The remedy for an accidental surplus of female population is female emigration, but this matter is to some extent self-regulating. Colonists want wives, and the more prosperous ones come back to fetch them. In the early days of the American and West India colonies, large numbers of women were sent out by the Government.

Polygamy prevails over three quarters of the world, and it is tolerated among two-thirds of the population of the British empire; but it is obviously an unnatural and inequitable institution, since the man who has four wives must hinder three men from having any. The marriage of a single pair is the only just marriage, and the rights of children and the interests of society require that it should be permanent.

Christian marriage, as defined by the Church, is the consent of a man and woman to become husband and wife. The formula is, 'I take thee', on the part of each. The priest, minister, registrar, or magistrate, is the legal witness of the mutual contract; but neither the ceremony in church, or the blessing of the priest, or his declaration, 'I pronounce you man and wife', constitutes the marriage. Even where marriage, as in the Catholic Church, is held to be a sacrament, the sacrament is not administered by the priest. It is equally a sacrament if witnessed by the registrar. Marriage is therefore the union itself, of man and woman, in mutual love, for the purposes for which such union exists – mutual help, and the propagation of the race. When the fact can be established as provided by the laws of each country, the marriage is considered valid, and the offspring legitimate.

Aside from inclination or vocation, there are many persons who should refrain from marriage. Persons afflicted with hereditary disease or deformity, and especially with tendencies to hereditary insanity, should not risk the propagation of such evils. There is little doubt that the tendency to drunkenness is hereditary, and there can scarcely be a greater curse than a drunken husband or wife, father or mother. Scrofulous and consumptive diseases run in families. The prospect of a short life, of children left orphans, perhaps destitute, and with the inheritance of hereditary disease, ought to deter many from marriage, much more than a mere lack of fortune.

At twenty-five, if established in life, or with a reasonable prospect of being able to support a family, a young man may think of marriage. If, in the society he frequents, he finds some person of suitable age, position, and attraction; one who, compared with all others, satisfies his judgment, as well as inspires his love; one for whom he feels that he can give up all other attractions; the one who meets him like destiny in the path of life; then let him frankly and honourably offer her those particular regards, those delicate attentions, which portend the offer of the heart.

And even now let him beware of any rashness or mistake. If he would be sure of the state of his own heart, he should wish to be no less sure of the real relation existing between him and the woman he would make his partner for life. In entering upon the indissoluble marriage of the church and the law that only crime or death can dissolve, great caution is requisite. Beware of surprising a woman who may be merely pleased with you, into an engagement she will feel bound to keep, however false. Beware of taking from benevolence or prudence what belongs to love.

Beware of the managing of matchmaking intermeddlers, and the importunities of relations – and especially beware of this, if you know yourself to be a desirable match in point of fortune and position. Beware of mistaking for love what may be but an approving taste; gratified vanity, or kindness of heart. Women are fatally misled by their benevolence. They yield to importunity, to pity, to the spirit of self-sacrifice. No man should ever accept a promise of marriage that is not given in perfect freedom and in perfect love.

A disappointment in love, the refusal of a lady, the desertion of a swain, is often followed on either side by a deplorable blunder. It is to accept hastily the next offer; to marry rashly, in a sort of revenge, as it seems sometimes, but more likely in search of consolation for a bitter disappointment.

Courtship is often, even though unintentionally, a series of deceptions. It is a period of hope and happiness. Both persons show their best and most amiable qualities, because they cannot help it. They are always dressed in their best – they look their best – they are on their best behaviour. There is a mutual hallucination, a haze of passion, which heightens every charm and conceals every defect. There is also a vanity which hastens the acceptance of an admirer, and hurries a courtship into an engagement. The servant maid flaunts her young man in the face of her fellows; the young lady is proud of having a beau; there is a feverish hurry to secure the prize of a settlement in life. Men are trapped; women are snared.

If a gentleman has made an engagement, it is not easy to withdraw. If he has proposed, and has been accepted, it is much the same as if he had challenged someone to fight, and the challenge was accepted. It remains for the challenged party to name time and weapons; and in case of an affair of marriage, it remains with a lady to name the happy day and the parson. But if either party becomes satisfied that it is a mistake, and that the marriage would therefore be misery for both, it is a solemn duty to withdraw, even if they were standing before the altar. Sometimes a man, expected to meet his bride at church, suddenly takes to flight. An expectant bride has eloped on the morning of her marriage with another. The thing to do is to throw one's-self upon the generosity of the other party, who should think it a happy escape. If the other party will not release you, still firmly refuse, and take the consequences. Whatever they may be, they cannot be so bad as a forced marriage.

When two persons have agreed to marry, there is usually some festive celebration of the event, needless here to describe, because it varies in different localities, and is well understood by the friends of the parties. The best man tutors the happy bridegroom, and guides him through the trying ceremony. The mother, or some matronly friend of the bride, helps her to fix the 'happy day', and gives her all the advice and instruction she needs. For those who regard marriage as a sacrament or solemn act of religion, the aid and counsel of priest or minister are sought and given. Roman Catholics go to confession, some spend several days in religious exercises and meditations, and they receive the holy sacrament of the Eucharist together at the marriage mass. Everything is done to give solemnity to the vows and act of marriage. There is no divorce, not even to save a kingdom.

The marriage vows are said; the marriage register signed; the irrevocable deed is done, the wedding breakfast eaten, its toasts drunk, its speeches made, the wedding presents inspected, and the old shoes thrown after the departing pair. In the lower ranks of life they go at once to the home prepared for them, and begin their married life. In the upper, they start off on a wedding tour, and spend the honeymoon in some favourite or fashionable resort.

I think the fashion of the humbler couple is the most sensible. A month of touring, of dissipation, of fashionable and expensive hotels, of utter isolation among strangers, does not seem to me a good beginning of married life. To enter upon the order, comfort, and delights of home, with sympathising friends, and society where it is agreeable, must surely be better for most people. The banishment of the honeymoon is too hard a trial.

Need I say how bridegroom and bride should behave to each other? Lovingly, of course, else why are they married? The husband is full of tender gallantry. The wife, all blushes, smiles, and tears, is full of hope and happiness, affection, and devotion. He has no thought but to 'love and cherish'; she none but to 'love, honour, and obey.' Henceforth it is the sole object of life in each to make the happiness of the other. Each has said, 'I take thee for better, for worse, for richer, for poorer, in sickness and health, till death do us part.' Each has said, 'With all my worldly goods I thee endow.' They are henceforth one heart, one body, with one property, one interest, one work in life. 'No more twain, but one flesh'; the symbol of the union of Christ and His Church. It is a very solemn mystery; and it might be well for husbands and wives to read over together at least once a-month the form of the contract into which they have entered.

The proper end of marriage, as I have already shown, is the production and rearing of offspring. The young of the animal races are quickly able to take care of themselves. Some need a few weeks or months of maternal care – the greater number, almost the whole marine and insect world, have no knowledge of their parents. But a human child requires parental care for years; and where there are several children their care, education, and establishment in life demand a lifetime, and therefore permanence in the marriage of their parents.

It is for each married partner to guard the health and secure the happiness of the other. The body of each is in the other's keeping. The husband cannot refuse anything to his wife, and the wife can seldom, and only in the interests of her offspring, refuse anything to her husband. Therefore there is so much the greater need of wisdom, prudence, and unselfishness on the part of each. From the first hour of possession, the husband is bound by every consideration of care, protection, love, and respect, to great delicacy, temperance, and at times entire continence toward his wife – first for her own sake, and next for the sake of his offspring. Marital rights exist only at natural periods. The higher demands and duties of maternity suspend them during gestation and lactation, as I have abundantly proved in portions of my scientific works specially devoted to these functions.

The health of thousands of men, tens of thousands of women, and of children innumerable, is wrecked by licentiousness in marriage. True love does not destroy its objects; but lust in marriage, as well as out of it, has a multitude of victims. I speak plainly, though briefly here, on this subject, and advise every reader, male or female, to thoroughly inform himself or herself, in regard to this most important subject in the science of life. I advise it the more urgently, because the world is full of errors respecting the relations of the sexes, and their duties to each other. So-called reformers, and even men who call themselves physicians, teach doctrines that tend to destroy all morality and all society.

Husbands and wives should live in mutual love and help, without waste of health or life, each considering the greatest good and happiness of the other. The rule is, that authority should be with the husband; obedience, in all things lawful, 'in the Lord', is the duty of the wife. But it is no less the duty of the husband never to require what the wife cannot and ought not to grant or do. Every service must be a reasonable service; every duty a reasonable duty; and, in the order of a true life, each should anticipate the proper demands of the other. If men and women could but carry through life the dispositions with which they stood together at the altar; if the life of marriage were but a continuance of the conciliations of courtship! This is perhaps too much to hope for – but here is the model for behaviour in marriage which every couple has in its beginnings.

In the family all property is in common, and there should be common industry. There is no reason why a man should be a slave to support wife and children in luxurious ease. The wife should at least be a thorough economist of the family income, if she cannot add to it. Marriage settlements may give security for the future; but the spirit of the marriage contract should never be violated.

And from the moment the contract is made between man and woman, there should be perfect faith – perfect trust in each other. No man should marry a woman in whose truth he cannot confide; no woman should give herself to a man whom she cannot trust utterly. This perfect trust in each other is expressed in the promise and contract of marriage. Jealousy is therefore the violation of plighted faith. No man should ever be jealous of his wife, for he should never allow the possibility to enter his mind that she can violate her solemn engagements. Jealousy is an accusation of bad faith, and we must be careful how we bring such accusations. To be jealous of another without cause, is one of the deepest injuries we can inflict. The author of *Realmah* says,

> If souls were visible there would be no jealousy, for we should find that the relation of any person for any other is so completely a relation between those two only, that there would be nothing for any third person to be jealous of.

But if there be cause, slight or grave, transient or permanent, it is right that each should try to recall the other to a sense of duty. There are the interests of children, friends, society. We must do as we would be done by, and forgive as we would be forgiven. Even if love be lost, scandal may be avoided, and much evil be averted by kindness and forbearance. At the worst there is private separation without clamour or disgrace. Men and women bear and forbear for the sake of their children. The broken faith may never be restored, but people can live together or live apart in mutual charity.

The laws afford no remedy. A man can sue the destroyer of his peace for damages – a sorry satisfaction and a great scandal – but a woman has not even this resource. The divorce court is open to both, though not on equal terms – but the divorce court is itself a public scandal and a source of demoralisation, and may become in time a nuisance that will have to be abated.

In a wise and true marriage all the wisdom of the head and all the instincts of the heart teach right behaviour to each other. Love, trust, help; generous confidence and generous forbearance; unvarying kindness, respect, politeness; a better manner to each other than either ever has to strangers – each seeking the other's good above all other considerations. Good men and women so living with each other thereby educate their children to the same course of life, and children both learn and inherit the virtues of their parents.

By the laws of most countries the legal existence of the wife is merged in that of her husband. The wife has no separate property, can make no contract or will, collect no wages, nor support herself. Her husband is bound to pay her debts, even those she contracted before marriage. She cannot sue or be sued. The wife must follow her husband, or stay at his bidding; live where he provides a home with no right to seek another. He owns her, and all that might else be hers, and has a supreme right over her children.

But when two are one, the supreme authority must centre somewhere, and it is best, on the whole, that it should be in the husband. If he is fit to be a husband he will not abuse his prerogatives. Really, the highest wisdom and the strongest will must govern. As a rule, those rule who can rule and ought to rule.

Work

The whole animal creation lives by work. The search and consumption of food is for many animals a busy industry. A great many work at building their habitations, and providing for their young. The industry of ants, and the business of bees and beavers, are our oft cited examples.

As the wants of man are greater than those of any other creature, so much greater must be his industry. He must cultivate the earth for his daily bread; his clothing, constantly wearing out, needs frequent renewal; he must have shelter from the inclemencies of climate; fuel to warm him and cook his food; beds, furniture, utensils, books, pictures, musical instruments – a thousand articles of necessity, use, or luxury.

All this involves work. The land must be cleared of its forests, broken up, and prepared for seed; the crops harvested, protected, threshed, ground, and prepared for food; linen and cotton raised, and wool sheared, silk gathered, leather tanned for clothing; wood and coal procured for fuel, and so on, with a vast amount of unceasing work, much of it wearisome, and some of it dangerous to health and life. That we may live and enjoy the comforts of civilisation, the land must be cultivated, and covered with flocks and herds; men must work in mines of coal, iron, copper, tin; there must be farmers, gardeners, millers, cooks, bakers, butchers; our dwellings employ stonecutters, brickmakers, masons, carpenters, plumbers, plasterers, painters, glaziers, cabinetmakers, upholsterers; for our clothing we have shoemakers, hatters, spinners, weavers, tailors, milliners, dressmakers, hosiers, glovers; our homes are full of the products of potters, glass workers, metal workers, jewellers, paper makers, bookbinders, workers in a hundred handicrafts, which make up the sum of human industry.

The world is full of work. It is the first duty of man. 'Work while it is called today.' 'If a man will not work neither shall he eat.' In a world where everyone lives on the products of labour, it is a matter of simple justice that everyone should do his share. The man who does not work lives upon the work of his neighbour. He gets food, clothing, shelter, comforts, and luxuries, for which he renders no equivalent. The idle man is a thief and a robber, shirking his share of the world's work. Somebody gathers his food, makes his clothes, builds his house, supplies his wants, and he does nothing in return.

In infancy, or old age, or sickness, we have the right of maintenance; but for an able-bodied man or woman to live in idleness on the toil of others, is a crying sin, a shameful injustice, an inhuman iniquity. Why should an able-bodied man be carried about on the back of another? Why should any man enslave his fellow man, and compel him to double toil to support him in idleness? But this is precisely what people are doing all around us. Slavery is the only kind we have ever abolished, and of that we have only changed the form.

It is not only the duty of every one to bear his proper share of the burthens of life, but it is his highest interest and happiness to do so. Labour is life – sloth is stagnation and death. What we call happiness is, in a great measure, the consciousness of duty done; of having been useful to others; of having promoted the welfare and happiness of those around us. Even our sports and pastimes, however useless or even mischievous and cruel they may be, simulate labour, and require exertion. Croquet, cricket, billiards, are a sort of work; so is riding a horse across country after a fox; and shooting and fishing involve as much muscular exertion as if they were useful employments. Work is so natural and necessary a thing, that we invent all sorts of make-believe industries, unproductive labours, and modes of spending our strength for naught, all the time living, perhaps in hurtful luxury and wasteful extravagance, upon the toil of those to whom we can render no equivalent, for no such equivalent is possible. We cannot give compensation for wasted life. For lives worn out in ceaseless toil to create the wealth we idly squander, what equivalent can we render?

It is a question of justice, of morality, of religion. Everyone should see it and feel it. Everyone should ask himself – What can I do that is best fitted to my capacities, and will be most useful to others? How can I best perform my duty to myself, my family, and the society to which I belong? The answer is plain enough. It is to earnestly engage in some useful work. It is to do with our might what our hands find to do. I think it would be well for everyone, of whatever position or calling, to labour with his hands some hours every day, like St Peter or St Paul, working in a garden or at some handicraft. It would be for the health and moral satisfaction of every one to earn his living. I have proved elsewhere that a man can live, as to his food, on sixpence a day, and I believe Abernethy was wise when he told his dyspeptic not only to live on sixpence a day, but to earn it. The man who has earned his living has not only the beautiful delight of the labour, but his conscience is at peace. He has borne his share of the burthen of life, done his part of the world's work.

In choosing our work, we must do what we can do best, and what most demands the doing. There are men born to follow the plough. It is their proud and happy vocation. Some men enjoy the care of horses and cattle, some love to work in mines, in forges, or as fishermen and sailors. Strong men enjoy the exercise of their strength, swift men, of their swiftness, cunning men, of their adroitness. Skilful men are for skilled labour; artistic men for art; intellectual men for investigation, invention, thought, imagination.

There is economy in the division of labour, and men should do the most of what they are best capable of doing. To put a born ploughman behind a counter, or employ a born artist as a cartman is bad economy. With freedom of choice and some opportunity for education, men would naturally seek and find suitable employments. But natural tendencies are warped by social prejudices. So long as idleness is considered a mark of gentility; so long as it is considered honest and honourable to live upon the labour of others; so long as high rank is given to low merit or to no merit whatever; so long as money, however obtained and however used, gives social position, great numbers of men and women will try to avoid work, and shrink from what they consider menial and degrading occupations. There is a constant effort to rise to what is considered a higher, that is, a more useless, position in life, and to live on the labour of others. Useful work is despised and therefore shunned. The labourer becomes an artisan, the artisan turns shopkeeper, the shopkeeper cheats, adulterates, puffs, speculates, invests, that he may retire from business, and live on the interest of his money – that is, on the labour of others. The producers of wealth have the ignoble ambition to become its distributors, and the distributors are constantly striving by dishonest gains to become its useless and burthensome consumers, because aristocracy has degenerated into idleness, and honour is divorced from use.

The time is coming when all this must be reformed; when men will be esteemed according as their lives are useful, and therefore honourable. Our present notions are barbaric. General education and a higher and truer civilisation will distribute the wealth and honours of society more equitably. Those who create wealth will be the first to enjoy its advantages – those who benefit mankind will stand highest in their esteem. It is the rule of heaven that everyone shall be rewarded according to his works. This is the will of God which we pray may be done on earth as it is in heaven.

Our right behaviour to our fellow men is that we find our best work and do it. The work we are best able to do, where demand is equal, is the best work for us. The basis work of all society is agriculture and gardening. As food is the first necessity of life, the supply of an abundance of healthy, nutritious and delicious food is the most important work, and therefore the most honourable. The culture of fruit was the first occupation of man, and it is still the most useful and the most delightful. It is natural and right that men should love the land, and enjoy the processes by which earth, water, air, and sunshine become vegetables, seeds, flowers, and fruits. If men should understand agriculture and gardening, still more should all women know how to cook. A certain proportion of the former may suffice, but there must be preparation of food in every family, and every mistress of a house, and everyone who may at any time be called to take charge of a house, should be practically acquainted with cookery.

The kinds of work next in importance are the making of clothing, and the building and furnishing, warming and ventilation of dwellings. Here are many kinds of useful employments, some of which require great skill and even genius. There was a time when queens span, wove, sewed, and embroidered the clothing of their households; when every wife made the clothing of herself and her husband, and every mother dressed her children; and no maiden thought of being married until she had manufactured her own trousseau, and the linen for her house. These beautiful employments have gone, and nothing has come to take their place. The maiden has nothing to show her lover but useless 'fancy work'; the most she can do for him is to embroider him a smoking cap or pair of slippers. Let us hope that we are in a transitional epoch, and that both men and women will soon find worthwhile work.

In the notes to 'Letter XXXIV' of *Fors Clavigera*, Mr Ruskin says,

A young lady writing to me the other day to ask me what I really wanted girls to do, I answered as follows:

Women's work is to please people, to feed them in dainty ways, to clothe them, too keep them orderly and to teach them.

I. To please; a woman must be a pleasant creature. Be sure that people like the room better with you in it than out of it; and take all pains to get the power of sympathy, and the habit of it.

II. Can you cook plain meats and dishes economically and savourily? If not, make it your first business to learn, as you find opportunity. When you can, advise, and personally help, any poor woman within your reach who will be glad of help in that matter; always avoiding impertinence or discourtesy of interference. Acquaint yourself with the poor, not as their patroness, but their friend: if then you can modestly recommend a little more water in the pot, or half an hour's more boiling, or a dainty bone they did not know of, you will have been useful indeed.

III. To clothe; set aside a quiet fixed portion of your time for making strong and pretty articles of dress of the best procurable materials. You may use a sewing machine; but what work is to be done (in order that it may be entirely sound) with finger and thimble, is to be your especial business.

First-rate material, however costly, sound work, and such prettiness as ingenious choice of colour and adaptation of simple form will admit, are to be your aims. Head-dress may be fantastic, if it be stout, dean, and consistently worn, as a Norman paysanne's cap. And you will be more useful in getting up, ironing, etc., a pretty cap for a poor girl who has not taste or time to do it for herself, than in making flannel petticoats or knitting stockings. But do both? And give – (don't be afraid of giving; Dorcas wasn't raised from the dead that modern clergymen might call her a fool) – the things you make, to those who verily need them. What sort of persons these are you have to find out. It is a most important part of your work.

IV. To keep them orderly, primarily clean, tidy, regular in habits; begin by keeping things in order soon you will be able to keep people also. Early rising, on all grounds, is for yourself indispensable. You must be at work by latest at six in summer and seven in winter (of course that puts an end to evening parties, and so it is a blessed condition in two directions at once.) Every day do a little bit of housemaid's work in your own house thoroughly, so as to be a pattern of perfection in that kind. Your actual housemaid will then follow your lead, if there's an atom of woman's spirit in her (if not, ask your mother to get another). Take a step or two of stair, and a corner of the dining room, and keep them polished like bits of a Dutch picture.

If you have a garden, spend all spare minutes in it in actual gardening. If not, get leave to take care of part of some friend's, a poor person's, but always out of doors. Have nothing to do with greenhouses, still less with hothouses.

When there are no flowers to be looked after, there are dead leaves to be gathered, snow to be swept, or matting to be nailed, and the like.

V. Teach – yourself first – to read with attention and to remember with affection, what deserves both, and nothing else. Never read borrowed books. To be without books of your own is the abyss of penury. Don't endure it. And when you've to buy them, you'll think whether they're worth reading; which you had better, on all accounts.

Very good as far as it goes. Every girl should learn and practice chiefly what she will need to know and do as wife, mother, mistress of a family, and in the care of children, of the sick, of the poor. She should learn every kind of work she may have either to do or direct. And in the uncertainties of life every girl, for her own dignity and safety, and to preserve her from dependence or the necessity of a false marriage, should be able to get her living as worker or teacher; by some useful craft or desirable accomplishment.

There is no lack of good employments for men. Every country needs good architects, capable of planning convenient, healthy, substantial, and beautiful dwellings, which are so rare, that vast numbers are greatly needed. Honest and capable workmen are wanted in every department of industry, and especially intelligent foremen and directors of the labour of others. Thousands of agricultural engineers, gardeners, horticulturists, and men acquainted with the care of poultry and bees could find employment. Men are needed who can increase the fertility of England, multiply its productions, and enhance its beauty. The great work of man is to subdue the earth, to cover it with fertility and beauty, and make it the home of an honest, prosperous, and happy society; and this can be done only by the union of genius, integrity, and industry – by the best kind of work.

Above all, honest work. Whether a man builds a house, or makes a coat, or writes a book, let it be done honestly, thoroughly, and as well as he can do it. The world is defrauded on all sides with tricks and shams. Theft is almost universal. Our bakers give us bad bread, milk is watered, groceries are adulterated, wines are poisoned, our tailors sell us shoddy, shoes fall in pieces, roofs leak, chimneys smoke, houses tumble in ruins about our ears. The greed of gain demoralises trade and industry. The man who sells any article which is not genuinely what it purports to be, steals. The man who takes more for anything than its fair and equitable value, steals. The man who exacts more than a fair compensation for his labour, as truly steals as he who picks your pocket. And there is the aggravation of bad faith, of deliberate and systematic deception. To think that a few years ago men were hanged in front of Newgate for stealing the value of a shilling!

SERVICE

In this world of work it is necessary to the order of society that some should oversee, direct, command, and that others should serve and obey. It is mutual service; for the brain serves the hands as well as the hands the brain. We all serve and are served. We have the civil service, military service, the naval service; Ministers of State are nominally Her Majesty's servants – really, the servants of the people. The ministers of religion, law, medicine, are public servants. Authors, journalists, artists, are but the most obedient humble servants of the community at large. Children are legally bound to render service to their parents until they are twenty-one years of age. Apprentices must serve their masters the appointed term; workmen and domestics, their employers. Tradesmen serve their customers.

The condition of a peaceful and prosperous society is faithful service. We want it everywhere, from highest to lowest. Woe to the State that is not served by able and faithful ministers; woe to the family which has stupid, disorderly, wasteful, and treacherous domestics. What can there be but misfortune, waste, want, and misery where politicians are selfish, clergymen negligent, lawyers dishonest, physicians ignorant and mercenary, tradesmen fraudulent, employers avaricious, workmen unfaithful, servants idle, pilfering, and disorderly? These are not accusations. I put the case in this way that every one may see the need of honest fidelity.

We must trust each other, and we must therefore be worthy of trust. We must trust our legislators for wise government, our judges to administer the laws, our soldiers to defend us, our police to watch and guard us. Everywhere is trust, and on every side is the liability to be cheated and betrayed, for we are all bound together – all members one of another. The human body is the type of human society. The perfection of society depends upon the completeness of its organisation, and the capacity and fidelity of its members. Perfect individuals will make a perfect society.

In every kind of service, whether to a master, captain, leader, or employer, there must be perfect honesty and fidelity. We have no more right to steal time than to steal money. Waste is theft. Negligence is theft. Unfaithful service is gross dishonesty. We may as well rob a man as to see another rob him without warning him, or doing our best to prevent it.

And in all service there should never be any question of pay or wages. Does a statesman serve his country for the salary he receives, and dole out his labour in proportion to the amount? Do legislators make laws because they are paid for it? Do clergymen regulate the performance of their duties by the value of their livings? Is a lawyer zealous in defence of his client in proportion to his fee? Does a physician or surgeon, by the bedside of a patient, ever think of pay? Has the soldier's sixpence a day anything to do with a desperate defence or a heroic assault on the field of battle? Do men volunteer in forlorn hopes with any thought of wages? Does a poet write, or an artist paint, or an orator speak according to his pay? Has the amount of salary anything to do with the efforts, the zeal, the enthusiasm and success of the musician, the singer, the actor? Why should it have, then, with the housemaid or cook, the labourer, the artisan, the mechanic, the assistant in any trade? Noble and generous souls have no mercenary motives. They do not consider equivalents. They work for the work's sake. Conscience and honour compel them to do good work. What their hands find to do, they do with their might.

Children must be sustained; apprentices properly provided for and taught; servants made comfortable; workmen equitably paid according to the value of their services, or according to their needs; but in no case is the amount of payment the real right motive for zeal and fidelity. To be mercenary is to be mean – on either side. All service should be free, voluntary, given from love of the work and love of those to whom it is rendered. And all reward should be of the same character – service for service. All spontaneous service is delight.

But this beautiful service of zeal and fidelity, this labour of love, must be reciprocal. Masters and employers must be just and generous, and as eager to reward service as they wish people to be to render it. A man who profits by the labour of others without giving fair value for it, is simply a robber. In every work which one person does for another there is a question of equity. The labourer is worthy of his hire. We must not muzzle the ox that treadeth out the corn. It is a matter of conscience with every master not to be indebted to any servant; not to stint him of his fair reward; to render unto every one according to his works; never to keep back the rightful share of any one in the proceeds of his labour. The agricultural labourer, for example, has a natural right to a comfortable dwelling, sufficient clothing, healthy food, education, recreation, and provision for the future; and no farmer has any right to profit, nor landlord to rent, until those who do the work have their rightful share of the products of their industry. It may not be possible to estimate to a penny what is a workman's or a servant's rightful share in any industry, but intelligent men can make a close approximation to an equitable compensation – and no honest workman will be willing to receive more, and no honest employer to give less. When two persons share an apple, each wishes to give the other the largest half. This is the generous rule in all dealings. Every servant should try to do more than is required, every master to pay more than simple justice demands. The master should say 'John, you are working too hard.' And John should say – 'Master, you are giving me more than I deserve.'

The rule of all service, high or low, is a generous, unselfish zeal, and an unswerving, unfaltering fidelity, on the part of the servant – on the part of those to whom service is rendered, a generous appreciation and unstinting reward, or giving service in return. This is the Christian rule of service. Everyone is bound to serve master or employer as he would serve God – with the same honest fidelity, generous zeal, and devotion. And the duties of masters to servants are of no less high moral and religious obligation.

Everyone can see how far service has fallen from this high standard. There is selfish greed and open war between employers and employed. It is, I believe, the consequence of carelessness, negligence, selfishness, oppression, and in many cases, inhuman cruelty on the part of masters and employers. There is a natural instinct of fidelity in men which responds to generous treatment. Good officers proverbially make good soldiers. Good masters have good servants. Service has been demoralised by the negligence or injustice of employers, until each is trying, not to do the best he can for the other, but the one to get the most work for the least wages, and the other to get the most wages for the least work. Masters combine together to keep down the price of labour – workmen combine to lessen the hours of labour and increase its price. The true way is for all to combine to find what is best for the interests of both and all classes.

I believe that the highest condition of mutual service is a system of free and generous co-operation – all working together for the good of all with an equitable division of the common wealth which is the result of industry. A fair and just distribution of this wealth would give everyone an abundance of all the necessaries, and many of the comforts and even luxuries of life. And this reign of justice would be the reign of peace, and society would rest upon a solid foundation. 'Honesty is the best policy.'

Need I say how masters and servants ought to behave in their personal intercourse with each other? We have the model of such conduct in patriarchal times, and rules for Christian masters and servants in the Epistles of the New Testament. A domestic servant is a member of the family, and to be treated with parental kindness and care. The servant owes respect, fidelity, a watchful care over the interests and character of the family. The old fashions in this matter are far better than the new. I know old people in England proud of having served in some good family for twenty or thirty years. In many churchyards may be read, 'for ... years the faithful servant of ...' The highest eulogy ever heard by man will be 'Well done, good and faithful servant.' I have no sympathy with those who wish to abolish the natural relations of master and servant. They are necessary to family life. Whatever changes and improvements we make in social organisation, the family must be preserved, and rather increased than diminished. But there can be no true family life while domestic servants are treated as if they were another race of beings; and they, finding no parental love and care, show no true respect, feel no affection, and practice no fidelity; but in every way deceive, betray, and plunder their employers. The rule of service is a ready obedience, order, cleanliness, cheerful alacrity, prudence, honesty, fidelity. Mercenary service, eye-service, slack, disorderly, wasteful and unfaithful service is the misery of domestic life; but I am convinced that the fault is mainly with masters and mistresses. No doubt servants demoralise each other, but people who know how to teach, train, and treat their servants will have good ones. The relation between a good master or mistress and a good servant is one of mutual comfort and delight. The test of good service is permanence. The rule of behaviour is the golden rule, which applies to all our relations and affairs. We should treat servants as we would be treated in their place; we should serve our employers as we would wish to be served.

TRADE

Why is trade looked upon as dishonourable, disreputable, and something which renders those engaged in it unfit for good society? Trade is a condition of civilisation. There can be no division of labour without exchanges. We buy and sell; buying is honourable, selling is base. What is the reason? Why should an idle, foolish, unmannerly cub, who never did one useful thing in his life, have his name in the court compartment of the Directory, and be received in society, while an intelligent, gentlemanly shopkeeper is excluded? Why is it proper to buy things but not proper to sell things? The highest lady in the land – the first gentleman in Europe may buy. Why would either lose caste by selling?

The reason is that trade is dishonest, and the taint of its general dishonesty attaches to all who engage in it. A nobleman may sell his horses or cattle – anything produced upon his estate; but if he were to buy for the purpose of selling again, he would become a tradesman, and be degraded from his nobility. He is tainted with the greed of gain, and the suspicion of rascality.

If trade were honest, it would never have become a reproach. A fair exchange of commodities is a gain to both parties, and honourable to both. The sole disgrace of trade is its dishonesty. Exchanges should be fair, just, equal. The man who takes more than the fair value of a thing, or gives less, defrauds his neighbour, and is guilty of the crime and sin of theft; and thieves cannot expect to be admitted into genteel society and have their names in the court side of the Directory.

But how, it will be asked, are we to get at the fair value and honest price of commodities? The price of a thing is whatever its possessor chooses to ask for it, or a purchaser is willing to pay. But a seller may be rascal enough to ask, and a buyer foolish enough to pay, three times its value.

Fancy prices are exceptional. Things that are rare or curious; old books, pictures, &c., bring prices at public auctions far beyond any intrinsic worth. A single bulb of a tulip has been sold for a thousand pounds. Gold and gems have a conventional and exchangeable value. The buying and selling value of a thing is what we can readily get in exchange for it in the open market. A bushel of wheat is worth certain quantities of barley, rice, potatoes, sugar, &c. A coat is worth a certain quantity of beef or apples. We put our prices in gold and silver, but only as a convenient means of exchange. Money represents articles of use or luxury. In the end, the exchangeable value of things depends upon their cost; the cost of things is the amount of labour expended in their production; and the honest price of a thing ought never to exceed a fair estimate of its cost.

If I buy a horse of a farmer who has raised him for fifty pounds, and sell him next day for a hundred, I have robbed somebody of fifty pounds. If the horse is worth but fifty pounds, I rob the man to whom I sell him. If he is worth more, I have robbed the farmer of whom I have bought him.

Anyone can see that a gentleman cannot go about stealing money from people in that way; and it is also easy to see that people who do such things are not gentlemen; and because tradesmen are constantly and systematically doing such things they are not considered gentlemen, and never can be until trade is reformed and made honest, and men carry into all their business the golden rule of all right doing.

The true principle of trade is equal exchanges. If one man raises an acre of wheat, and another an acre of potatoes, with equal labour, and the produce is 60 bushels of wheat and 180 bushels of potatoes, then each bushel of wheat may be fairly exchanged for three bushels of potatoes. Cost is the limit of price. Where cost cannot be estimated, we may take value. A pound of wheat may be equal in nutritive value to five pounds of potatoes; but we give more than things are really worth as nutriment, to gratify our palates, and for the sake of variety.

Of course the time or labour of those who distribute articles enters into the cost, and a pound of tea passes through several hands between the Chinaman who raises it and gets perhaps a penny a pound for it, and the English consumer who pays three shillings. The man who raises grapes in the south of Spain may get sixpence for as many as will make a bottle of wine, which sells in England for ten shillings. The nine-and-sixpence are divided in this way – labour in making, transporting, and selling, eighteen-pence; profit, eight shillings.

All honest trade is frank, open, and above-board. No honest man will hesitate to tell what any article has cost him, and to let the purchaser know what he is paying him for his services in selling it I have as much right to know what I give a man for selling me a yard of cloth, as for making a jacket. A tradesman has a right to a fair price for the service he renders me, and to no more. It is a part of the cost. Profit, or a price above a fair compensation for service rendered, is a fraud upon the purchaser; and as people get their eyes open to this, they will more and more combine together to get honest exchanges and throw off the burthen of paying profits which enrich some, and support great numbers in idleness.

The rule of all trade should be to mark every article with its actual cost to the dealer, and then with the price for which he is willing to sell it. This would be fair to seller and buyer. The cost mark should be as much subject to legal investigation as are weights and measures. It is the right of every one who buys to get honest measure, honest weight; and it is just as much his right to get things of honest quality and at an honest price.

There was once, and perhaps still is, a country in the heart of Europe where people left their little shops to keep themselves. The goods were all marked with their prices, and customers came and helped themselves to what they wanted, putting the pay in the till; and there was no thought that anyone would cheat or steal. That is good behaviour.

There is a fair and honest price for every man's labour, which every fair and reasonable man is willing to pay. We respect the man who asks this honest price, and we despise, and perhaps detest, the man who asks us more. We may bear the exaction, but we have no good feeling toward those who cheat and rob us. When trade is made honest, it will become honourable.

The moral and religious principles involved in this matter are very important. We can have no true society until we have settled this question of trade. There can be no real social enjoyment between people who are preying upon each other. We might as well surround ourselves with pilferers and pickpockets as with people who take every occasion to cheat us. Getting the best end of a bargain is only a mode of theft. The Catechism will tell us that we are bound to make restitution for every wrong. It was not for nothing that Christ drove the traders and money changers out of the temple. They had made it a 'den of thieves', but there is no reason to believe they were worse than the drapers and grocers who sell shoddy for cloth, chicory or burnt sugar for coffee, and everything for the highest profit they can get of the needy and ignorant.

There is a movement wide and deep in favour of honest dealing – at least, for protection against the frauds and rapacities of trade. Co-operation will undermine and destroy it, unless it become honest. The more intelligent the community becomes, the less will it be possible to make people endure the outrageous frauds and pay the enormous profits of unscrupulous commerce.

How should tradesmen behave to their customers? Need I say respectfully? Most tradesmen are civil enough to those whose custom is desirable. They are obsequious to people of rank and fashion, but I have seen tradesmen who were insolent and abusive to their humbler customers; and many are pertinacious and annoying in their efforts to induce people to purchase. A shopman should be polite, but not obtrusive; he should show his wares rather as if to give pleasure and gratify curiosity, and in friendly helpfulness, than to persuade people to buy what they do not need. He should avoid exaggeration, and never tell an untruth. To lie for gain is the meanest of all lying; and because there is a general belief that tradesmen lie, there is a feeling that a tradesman cannot be a gentleman.

But a tradesman who wishes to be really honest, and do as he would be done by, in trade as in everything else, must not only not lie – he must speak the truth. He cannot honourably withhold or conceal it. What would be thought of a gentleman who should sell a horse without telling the purchaser its faults? He might as well pass a bad sovereign. And I am sure that in this matter, as in all others, honesty is the best policy; and that the best thing any dealer could do in the long run, would be to tell the exact truth about every article; and if it was poor, or imperfect, dear, or undesirable in any way, to frankly say so. The true policy of every tradesman is to so treat all persons as to gain their confidence and respect. To do this he must be polite, frank, honest, unselfish, and high above all tricks and subterfuges, considering the interests of his customers quite as much as his own, and in all ways dealing with them fairly and equitably.

The man who asks too much for an article defrauds the buyer. The man who takes less than he asked at first, confesses that he intended to defraud him. The man who trusts a doubtful customer should take the risk upon himself. He has no right to average bad debts on cash or paying customers, unless they agree to this system of mutual insurance.

How should tradesmen behave to each other? Assuredly only in one way – as neighbours and friends. With honest dealing there would be an end of competition and opposition. No man has a moral right to open a shop or set up a business which will injure one already engaged in it. In some countries the laws will not permit such opposition. And why should a man go to work deliberately to take the bread out of the mouth of another? I cannot see how it differs from felony. In certain trades, the liquor trade, for example, the law regulates the number and places of dealers. Magistrates license only as they judge that the public needs the accommodation. For a tradesman to set himself down in a neighbourhood with the deliberate design of getting away the business of a' worthy man already established, perhaps with a family dependent on him for support, is an atrocity beyond the usual crimes of highwaymen and pirates. Tradesmen should be honest to each other, but when they combine to impose exorbitant prices upon the public, they are simply a band of robbers, and it is not only the right but the duty of the public to combine against them.

No man should engage in any business which is not useful to the public, or, at least, harmless. No man has the right to make or sell what will injure the health, property, or morals of the people. If it can be shown that any trade does more harm than good, no man should engage in it. Yet a large part of the revenues of this country are drawn, and a great capital engaged, and many thousands employed in the manufacture

and sale of ardent spirits and tobacco, which, in the opinion
of a great number of persons, are almost unmixed evils. It will
not be disputed that drunkenness is in this country a fruitful
cause of poverty, ignorance, vice, crime, and misery. Drink
makes drunkards. Drunkards become paupers, abuse and
sometimes murder their wives, neglect their children, and are
in many ways a burthen to society. Every tradesman should
be a benefactor and a blessing – is not a tradesman who aids
in the manufacture of drunkards a malefactor and a curse?

I do not know how the publisher who makes, and the dealer
who sells, pernicious books can be justified in injuring society
for gain. It may be said that they supply a demand of the
public; but have they a right to supply such a demand? There
are demands we have no right to satisfy. The truth is that they
often create the demand. The bad book is advertised, puffed,
pushed into circulation. I think a bookseller should no more
sell or circulate a demoralising story than tell one.

How can men justify the making of enormous fortunes
by the manufacture and sale of quack medicines – that is, of
preparations which cost almost nothing to make, and have no
value as remedies, and are in some cases injurious. They are sold
by large expenditures of money in the publication of stupendous
falsehoods to impose upon the credulous and ignorant. A
shilling box of pills costs a halfpenny; a five shilling bottle costs
three-pence. The rest is distributed among the newspapers and
printers that advertise, the dealers that sell, and the proprietor
who lays up a fortune gathered from the poor, and who may
perhaps found a hospital for their benefit. What can be said of
the honesty of such a proceeding? Granting that there is good
faith in the pretence of the efficacy of the nostrum, how can we
justify the price at which it is supplied?

The law of trade is honest usefulness – doing genuine service
to the public, and asking only a just reward. When trade comes
to this standard it will become honourable.

SPECULATION

Ought a man to speculate – that is, to run great risks in order to get great gains? Ought a man to gamble? All speculation is gambling. It is a game of chance, or a game of skill, or the two combined. We gain or lose by accident – circumstances beyond our knowledge or control; or by superior knowledge or craftiness. In every case, our gain is dependent upon another's loss; our fortune is somebody's misfortune. We get what was not ours, for which we have rendered no equivalent.

It may be a small matter – a pleasant excitement to sit round a table and risk, lose, or win a few shillings or pounds, playing with cards or dice. In England many thousand persons, of all classes, from princes to beggars, make wagers on the national games of races – a system of gambling more widespread than exists elsewhere in the world, and one involving more fraud and crime than any other. The public gaming tables at the pleasure resorts of Germany have been abolished by law. There is no sign of such abolition of turf gambling in England, though there are laws against certain forms of betting. Lotteries are abolished – art unions are authorised, and gambling for charity and religion tolerated.

But the principle of speculation or gambling is everywhere. The whole credit system in trade is gambling, risking money on the contingencies of the life, health, honesty, or ability of those we trust. We buy property or merchandise in the hope that it will increase in price. We buy stocks, or public securities, hoping that political events will raise, or we sell on time, on the chance that some calamity may depress them. Men speculate in corn or cotton, and sometimes combine to raise or depress prices, and so make fortunes. It is evident that all such speculation is simply gambling, and that it is sometimes robbery as well. The cards are marked – the dice are loaded. The man who attempts to influence the event on which he risks his money loads the dice – he might as well pick a pocket. Where all are doing their utmost to win, you may say it is a fair game. The weakest goes to the wall. It is only a greedy scramble, and those who win and those who lose are equally guilty. The essence of gambling and of all kinds of speculation is the desire and effort to get what does not belong to us, what we have no right to, what we have never earned, that for which we render no equivalent.

Probably the least objectionable form of gambling is the lottery, where the risks are small, and made at regular periods, and the contributions of great numbers make up the prizes. But lotteries were abolished in England by Act of Parliament, because it was found that the system was demoralising alike to winners and losers. Those who lost grew more greedy of unearned gold – those who gained squandered their ill-gotten wealth in dissipation and vice.

The only kind of gambling which meets with general favour is the assurance of property, health, or life. I make a wager, at long odds, that my house will take fire, that my ship will founder or be wrecked, that I shall fall ill, or be disabled by some accident, or that I shall die before a certain period. This is a lottery, in which the contributions of many persons compensate for the calamities of the few. Men sometimes set their houses on fire, or send off unseaworthy ships, or bribe captains to sink them, to get the insurance; but the principle of mutual help is beneficent. What is not right is, that a large portion of the money contributed is swallowed up in wasteful management, or distributed among shareholders. All insurance should be done by government, and at bare cost to the whole body of the insured – any margin of profit going to diminish taxation. There is no reason why numbers of people should draw revenues from the misfortunes of their fellow citizens.

All modes of 'making money' fall under the head of speculation or gambling. No money, or money's worth, is ever made but by human labour, skill, or genius. Making money is getting possession of it by chance, or fraud, or some mode of compulsion; and differs in no way, as to its morality, from theft or robbery. It is taking it without rendering anything in return. Thus we pay large sums of money to people who have seized upon our rivers and make us buy our water. Other companies have been permitted to tax us heavily for gas, and hundreds of families live in luxury on what we are obliged to pay beyond its cost. The stores of fuel laid up in the bowels of the earth, so many thousands of years ago, have fallen into the hands of individual appropriators, who combine to exact millions from the avarice of the rich, and the necessities of the poor. The land of these islands is in the possession of a few families, and every atom of food contributes to their revenues. Its price is also enhanced by the interest paid every year for money squandered centuries ago in wars. The very highways of the country – our means of passage and transport – have been given up to private companies, who tax the public for their own emolument.

Investments in public companies are generally, perhaps always, in the nature of speculation or gambling. There is the risk of loss – there is the hope of gain; and for a portion of this gain, at least, we render no equivalent. If we buy stock in water, gas, mining, or railway companies, we may idly consume the money gathered from exorbitant prices. Every penny above an accurately just price asked for service rendered is stolen, and the receiver is as bad as the thief. Really, a stockholder in any company which robs the people is a member of a gang of thieves.

That a man should receive a fair price for the use of land or buildings, tools or money, which he has rightfully acquired, I shall not here deny. The government of this country pays depositors in the Post Office Saving's Banks two-and-a-half per cent interest; it pays the holders of the public debt three per cent. If these are honest rates, what are we to think of companies that divide ten, twenty, thirty per cent, among their stockholders? When a man hires money at three per cent, and turns round and lends it, as money lenders sometimes do, for five or ten times as much, how is one to draw the line between open robbery and such transactions?

We can imagine all the land of a country in the hands of a single proprietor, or a great joint stock company, and people paying heavy rents under pain of starvation; or all the coal belonging to one owner who could levy any tax on labour in payment for fuel; or a combination of speculators in corn or cotton to double the prices of bread and clothing; but will anyone pretend that open robbery would not be quite as honest and humane?

The rule of a true life is the rule of justice. As far as possible we should in no way participate in oppression or dishonest gain. There were formerly people in England who would not eat slave-grown sugar, nor wear slave-grown cotton; and it would be well if no one would eat, wear, or use any thing for which a full and honest price had not been paid to the labourers who produced it. Unrequited labour is slavery; and this slavery of unrequited labour is the source of all dishonest gains.

PROFESSIONS

The choice of a profession is determined by circumstances, aptitude, talents, or vocation. Men who fill professions come generally from the upper and middle classes. They must have the means of acquiring a good education at least, and in most cases, some help in the beginning of their career. They should have a special liking for, and adaptation to, the work they purpose to do, the talents necessary for success, and in some cases a special call or interior attraction for their particular work.

Every profession is a kind of service. Thus we speak of the military service, the naval service, the civil service. Professional men serve the public at large rather than particular individuals. The clergyman serves his parish, the lawyer his clients, the physician his patients, yet people say: My medical man, my legal adviser. Soldiers serve their country. It is service everywhere.

Every clergyman is supposed to have a vocation. In the Roman Catholic Church the clergy are trained from childhood, and their vocations carefully tried, up to the time of their ordination at the age of twenty-five years. Vows of celibacy mark their devotion to a peculiar function to which they believe themselves supernaturally called. In Protestant countries the clergy have neither the same kind of training for their work, nor the same separation from worldly motives and interests. An English clergyman generally has a wife to please, children to educate, sons to start in life, daughters to marry. Church livings are a part of the property of wealthy families, and the church is chosen as a profession from worldly as well as unworldly considerations.

Socially considered, the clerical profession is one of great importance. The clergy are the educators of the whole body of the people. They have such opportunities, public and private, as belong to the members of no other profession. It is their business to teach, exhort, admonish, advise, and direct.

Every week, it may be several times a week, they speak to people on the most important concerns of life. They are welcome visitors to every household. They christen, catechise, marry, comfort, console. Young and old go to them with their troubles and trials, their sorrows and their sins. No men have such advantages or such responsibilities.

Therefore a clergyman should be a man of men, 'thoroughly furnished for every good word and work'. He has but one business in life – the service of his fellow creatures. He is the shepherd of the flock, not one of which must be lost by his incompetency or neglect. Especially is he the guide of the ignorant and the guardian of the poor, the exponent of justice, the exemplar of charity, the almoner of bounty. There is no limit to the good which an able, zealous, devoted clergyman may accomplish. He stands between God and men, between the rich and the poor, between the oppressor and the oppressed. He can say what no other man can say, he can do what no other can do. Every clergyman has his models and examples in Christ and his Apostles. He has only to ask himself – what would they say, what would they do in my place? He has the record of what they taught and what they did. How earnest were all their words, how noble were all their deeds!

Surely, of all men, a clergyman should be the most free from selfish, worldly, mercenary consider actions. Only a high sense of duty, a call of God to be His minister, could induce any one to take upon people of England should at once demand new economies and regulations for land and mines. Food, coal, and iron are too precious things to be handed over to the greed or indolence of speculators and proprietors. These things lie at the basis of national progress and happiness.

Justice here, is the foundation of the higher civilization, the better social condition, to which we aspire and for which we labour. A law of compensation for improvements would so increase the fertility of England and its prosperity, as to settle at once all the troubles of the agricultural labourers, and greatly improve the condition of artisan populations. Every peer, and every member of the House of Commons, every publicist and journalist, should study this question of the land, and of natural wealth and its administration. The national legislature is the depository, guardian, and administrator of the national domain, and all its riches and capabilities. Property depends on law. Those who make can unmake. Just laws are the economies of a nation. As the people become enlightened, and suffrage is more extended, the more urgently will there be a demand for wise legislation. If the hereditary aristocracy neglect its high functions, it will be relieved from them. The Church will not be disestablished, nor the House of Lords abolished, by any exterior force; but both may wither, and perish, and be swept away when they no longer perform the duties for which they were constituted. Practical people want that we may conquer all our enemies in the battle of life.

The profession of the Law is one of great dignity. Judges, barristers, solicitors, and attorneys are ministers of justice, guardians of right and equity, defenders against every sort of oppression and wrongdoing. It is the entire business of every lawyer to see that truth prevails and justice triumphs. He has to defend the innocent, and punish the guilty, and justice can never be a question of money. We have a legal profession, with all its honours and emoluments, in order that the poorest man shall be as secure of his rights as the richest. No honest lawyer looks at the wealth of a client, or considers the amount of a fee. Justice is a thing too holy for mercenary considerations. A clergyman might as well preach, as a lawyer plead, for money.

But a lawyer, it may be said, must defend unjust causes and guilty men. There is no such must. He is bound to do what any honourable man should do for another from motives of justice and charity. You have a just claim; I will help you to gain it. This is an unjust demand; I will aid you in resisting it. The law is for the protection of rights; it is the embodiment of justice; the formulation of common-sense. Therefore a lawyer, of whatever degree, and everyone who is the minister of the law, from the Lord Chancellor to the policeman, is bound to act according to the principles of justice and equity.

If a cause is evidently unjust, an honest lawyer must say so to his client. If it is uncertain, he must help him to find out the truth. That is what he is for. It was never intended that men should make a profession of supporting injustice.

The judge is no more obliged to impartial equity, than every barrister and solicitor. The lawyer who aids injustice is an accomplice; he who attempts to screen a felon is *porticeps criminis*. All that an honourable man can do is to see that the defence is fairly heard.

It is needless to say how far these principles have been lost sight of, and how far the legal profession has been prostituted to the defence of fraud and wrong, until men are warned to avoid law as they would ruin; and we are advised to try arbitration and conciliation. But this is precisely the intention of the law itself; and every court, civil and criminal, should be a place where ever one, poor or rich, could go with the security of getting free and speedy justice. It is the first principle of law and government that there must be a remedy for every evil, a way to right every wrong. And this way should be made perfectly easy, safe, practical, and costless to the person aggrieved. The profession of the law exists for one sole object – that justice may be done, and communities live in the peaceful enjoyment of their rights.

Medicine is a far more difficult profession than law. Its intent is simple enough, but its principles and modes are not so easily settled. The object of the land, and pays all interests and dividends on capital.

Wealth, recently acquired, is the sign of talent, energy, greed, craftiness, perhaps of utter selfishness and crime. A millionaire may be a clever and successful gambler, whose success has impoverished thousands. Not much can be said of an aristocracy of financiers, speculators, or of men in any kind of business who merely make money. The worship of wealth, no matter how acquired, is one of the basest of human infirmities. The fact that money will buy a church living, a seat in Parliament, admission to good society, an honourable matrimonial alliance, is a very shameful one. A purse-proud aristocracy is very despicable – but those who are ready to sell themselves for gold are more to be despised than those who are ready to buy them. The pride of wealth is base, the worship of wealth is contemptible.

Honour to whom honour is due. Render unto Caesar the things that are Caesar's. The true aristocracy – the best men and the best women of the nation – are honourable and right honourable. All worth, all merit, all excellence is worthy of honour and reward. Good men and good women on earth, and saints in heaven, have a just claim upon our reverence. It is a virtue to appreciate virtue, honourable to honour it. If we cannot live a true life, it is something to say amen to it – something to admire it and glorify it. We seek what we love, we emulate what we admire. Let us cherish then every of the clergyman to teach morals and religion. Then anyone who became ill by his own act, or by any disregard of the laws of health, should be liable to fine or fee; and anyone who, by his bad habits of living, introduced any epidemic or contagious disease, should be severely punished. Every farmer can see what a man would deserve who should so treat his stock as to originate cattle disease; or who should introduce it into any neighbourhood. If medical men were employed by the State, they could be called to account for an increased death-rate. There is no doubt that the mortality of the whole United Kingdom could be reduced to the standard of the healthiest districts. A death-rate of thirty in a thousand means the needless slaughter of multitudes of our population, which will some day be looked upon with the same horror as that with which we shudder in reading of the customs of Ashantee or Dahomey.

Members of the medical profession have need of great tolerance and courtesy toward each other; the more, perhaps, because there is no established system of orthodoxy in medical science or practice. The Church claims the power to settle controversies in matters of faith. Parliament makes laws, and the Courts settle rules of practice; but there is no authority or standard in medicine, and every practitioner is free to prescribe whatever he may think best for his patients. Allopathists, homeopathists, hydropathists, and medical eclectics are on the same level of equal rights before the law, and people who have no knowledge of medical science have to choose as they best can the doctors who shall attend them. Happily all sorts of doctors cure their patients, or their patients recover in about the same proportions. I am disposed to think that the man is more important than the medicine, and that moral influence is of more efficacy than drugs. Faith, hope, confidence, expectation, are energising and purifying agencies.

If physicians owe tolerance, courtesy, and all sorts of friendly aid to each other, their duties to society, and to those who call upon them for their services, are also very clear. Whatever a man knows, he is bound to make practically useful. It can never be a question with a true man, or any one worthy of the name of a physician – how shall I be paid? One might as well stand by the sea and consider whether a drowning man could pay for being pulled out of it. Fancy a surgeon allowing a man to bleed to death because he doubted whether he could pay for taking up an artery. It would be murder; and the same rule applies to all medical practice. A man really owes all the service he can render to his fellow men; and certain professions are called honourable, and those practising them are considered gentlemen, because they are not mercenary. No clergyman, no barrister, no physician can take pay for the performance of his professional duties. The service is spontaneously rendered – what we give is an honorarium, an offering, freely bestowed. No question is asked – the honorarium is delicately wrapped in paper and unobtrusively left where it may be found. The reason why all professional men refuse to mix up pecuniary matters with their work is, that money, as the representative of selfish greed, debases all it touches. Love is not bought or sold, and all true service should be loving service; commanding, but never demanding, love and service in return. It should be given as promptly to the poor as to the rich. In religion, law, and medicine, all are equal. If God is no respecter of persons, neither should be His ministers, nor the ministers of justice and health.

There is a social sacredness, so to speak, about these three professions. Clergymen, lawyers, and physicians are in the secrets of thousands of persons and families. All hear confessions, and all are bound by the sacred seal of the confessional. The clergyman who should betray the confidence of a penitent, the lawyer who should reveal the secrets of a client, or the doctor those of a patient, would be considered infamous. They are privileged communications. Neither can be compelled, even on the witness stand, to give them up. Such relations are high above all considerations of pounds, shillings, and pence.

And all professions have more or less of this noble, unselfish and unpecuniary character. No man goes into the military or naval service for his pay. He gives his time, his talents, his life, if need be, to serve his country. Therefore an officer is a gentleman, and every soldier ought to be a gentleman also. The treatment of private soldiers in England is infamous, perhaps because, owing to the system of enlistment, the character of too many of the men has been infamous also. If the government had a standard of character for the military service, as well as one for height and physical efficiency, the uniform would be a badge of honour instead of one of inferiority and disgrace. It is a disgrace to England that a private soldier or non-commissioned officer, with good conduct stripes upon his arm and heroic medals on his breast, is refused admission to some of the most popular places of amusement. The French, German, or American soldier can go everywhere, and in some cases has special privileges.

Architecture, civil engineering, painting, sculpture, music, and the drama are professions daily rising into higher honour and esteem. Architects, artists, and musicians have had the honours of knighthood. I do not remember that any actor has been knighted, but there is no reason why a Garrick or a Kemble, a Kean or a Macready should not be. There are few who would refuse any honour to William Shakespeare or Ben Johnson. And why should not similar honours be given to a Mrs Siddons, a Miss O'Neil, a Patti, or a Nillson?

I have left the professions of education and literature to the last; but they are not the least useful and honourable. The professors of universities and masters of English high schools are highly honoured – but the teachers of the common and primary schools of the country are not treated with the consideration that their functions merit. The schoolmaster should take rank close beside the clergyman. Parents should treat him with respect as one to whom they have delegated their authority and duties. Teachers and governesses are not upper servants. Their functions are not mechanical or mercenary. They are intellectual, moral, and affectional. They cannot be paid for in money;

they demand unpurchaseable qualities of head and heart – qualities that should be esteemed and honoured. When a parent confides a child to the care and culture of tutor, governess, or teacher, he should show for either of them the respect and consideration which ought to be impressed upon the pupil; and no child should ever be entrusted to the care of any one not worthy of such respect.

Authors are the educators of the race. Some poets, historians, essayists have been the delight of a hundred generations. A man of genius influences the thoughts and lives of hundreds of millions of men. What do we not owe of honour and gratitude, and such reward as we can give, to those whose writings have made us wiser and happier! The rule of all professional life holds here with a force in proportion to the importance of the work. If the clergyman is bound to teach no error in doctrine or morals; if the lawyer is bound to aid in no injustice; if the first rule of medicine is to do no harm; the author is equally obliged to never violate the principles of pure taste and sound morality. Better raise good wheat than write a bad book. Better get one's living as a tinker, than corrupt the morals and lower the tone of society by a vicious literature.

Journalism is a distinct and very important profession, of so recent a date, however, that its position is scarcely defined. But the province and duties of a journalist are evident enough. It is to publish the truth from good motives and for justifiable ends. It is to enlighten and educate the public in what most concerns its welfare. The journalist should be unselfish, unprejudiced, liberal, wise, generous, and philanthropic. He should be a gentleman in all his tastes and feelings; humane, courteous, just, chivalric; scorning a mean action, prompt to recognise a good one; the prudent censor of vice, the unhesitating denouncer of corruption. Every kind of merit he should eagerly praise, and educate the public taste, and improve art and literature, by generous and impartial criticism. How pure and true, how just and honourable, how free from every taint of selfishness or vanity, greed for glory or greed for gain, should be the man who conducts a public journal which may have its thousands or its hundreds of thousands of daily readers! In no profession is honesty, integrity, the highest kinds of practical wisdom and virtue more needed. The bad clergyman may have no influence beyond his parish; the mischief making lawyer works in a shorten the lives of a few patients. But an unprincipled journalist is a national calamity. He may demoralise society, overturn a government, foment insurrections, and be the cause of incalculable evils, crimes, and miseries.

ARISTOCRACY

Every country has its aristocracy – its best people, who always ought to govern the rest. Where there is universal suffrage, they influence and control that mode of expressing public opinion. Forms of government are therefore of little importance. The wisdom and strength of a nation are its real government, however it be administered.

In the nature of things, an aristocracy is hereditary. Certain qualities of force, genius, power to order and command, descend from father to son. Beauty, grace, wisdom, and goodness also distinguish families through many generations. We have these distinctions of blood and breeding as notable in men and women as in dogs and horses. Education and culture may bring us all to higher standards, but the differences will remain. There is no probability of uniformity, nor is it desirable. It would be a terrible monotony. When every man has the best development of which he is capable, there will still be a wide scale of diversities and gradations.

The desire for success in life, for distinction, esteem, approbation, honour, and fame is entirely natural, and a condition of progress. It is right that everyone should strive to better himself, and improve his condition – right that parents should try to raise their children to a higher level than their own – provided that this can be done without injustice, and that it involves no depression of others. If every man were to leave his land more fertile and beautiful than he found it, his dwelling more elegant and commodious, his children better educated than himself, and all about him more prosperous and happy for his life and work, there would be true progress.

There is no gain in hoarding wealth; no gain in acquiring land; but the man who can double the productiveness of his land is a general benefactor. He increases the wealth of the country as well as his own. He draws it from the inexhaustible supplies of air and sunshine. The improvement of the soil of a country is one of the highest duties of its inhabitants, and every acre of land should be so held that it can do its utmost for human happiness. The import of vast quantities of food from other countries is a disgrace to this. The land is here that might produce it, the labour is here waiting to be employed. The means of enriching the earth are washed into the seas. Farmers will not improve their land because they have no security.

And what, the reader may ask, has all this to do with behaviour? Everything. The good behaviour of the aristocracy that must always govern, is to govern wisely and well; and the land of every country must be the first care of its rulers. The land is the nation's heritage – its means of life. Every man born into the world has a natural right in the land, on which he must live, or by whose productions he must be fed, as much as to the air he must breathe. The earth belongs to man as well as the atmosphere, the blue sky and sunshine, clouds, moon, and stars. The land and the utmost of its productiveness, and the treasures it conceals, are the common property of men, of which no man can be justly deprived. The laws of England concede the minimum of this universal right, in the Poor Law, which guarantees food, clothing, and shelter to all. It is the duty of legislators to secure to all men the maximum of this right by so regulating the possession and use of land as to ensure its highest productiveness, and the just distribution of all its wealth. The people of England should at once demand new economies and regulations for land and mines. Food, coal, and iron are too precious things to be handed over to the greed or indolence of speculators and proprietors. These things lie at the basis of national progress and happiness.

Justice here, is the foundation of the higher civilization, the better social condition, to which we aspire and for which we labour. A law of compensation for improvements would so increase the fertility of England and its prosperity, as to settle at once all the troubles of the agricultural labourers, and greatly improve the condition of artisan populations. Every peer, and every member of the House of Commons, every publicist and journalist, should study this question of the land,

and of natural wealth and its administration. The national legislature is the depository, guardian, and administrator of the national domain, and all its riches and capabilities. Property depends on law. Those who make can unmake. Just laws are the economies of a nation. As the people become enlightened, and suffrage is more extended, the more urgently will there be a demand for wise legislation. If the hereditary aristocracy neglect its high functions, it will be relieved from them. The Church will not be disestablished, nor the House of Lords abolished, by any exterior force; but both may wither, and perish, and be swept away when they no longer perform the duties for which they were constituted. Practical people want the worth of their money. They count the cost of things, and dispense with the useless, and cast away the pernicious. A nobleman who sees what he is for, and tries to do his duty in that station in life to which he is called, will be a noble man always. True leaders of men are too precious to be thrown aside. We want them – everyone. Devotion to a genuine aristocracy is one of the strongest instincts of humanity. We look about for leaders, we up with poor ones for the lack of better; but our leaders must lead. There is no lack of hero-worship, and no danger, but from lack of heroes to worship. Since we must have an aristocracy, let it be of the best. Genius makes its own way and rules in its own fashion. We all recognise and bow down to it. We read its poems and novels; we delight in its works of art; we glory in its achievements. This Aristocracy is beyond all law, and its rank is in the hearts of men. Genius moulds opinion and gives it power. It makes the songs of all people; and those who sing them make the laws. Genius is the power to perceive Truth and create Beauty. It governs in its own right.

The aristocracy of talent or practical aptitude is a larger body, and the supply is more constant. It reigns in all the professions, governs business, organises politics and philanthropy, and takes an active, leading part in all the affairs of life. Its faults are short-sighted selfishness and proneness to routine. It runs in ruts and follows precedents; while genius makes them and disregards them.

What we call the Aristocracy of wealth is a misnomer. No one pretends that rich men are the best men; but wealth is power, and an indication of talent or force of character in those who have gained it. Wealth is the accumulation of the results of labour in the hands of those who have been able to gather and keep it. It is a congestion. In a true social state there would be a free and equable circulation of all the goods of life – the bountiful nourishment of every part. In the actual condition of society some are gorged and some are starved. It is an unnatural, diseased, morbid condition. In the nature of things, all great gatherings of wealth in the hands of individuals must have begun in spoliation. They are essentially unjust. In these islands the lands have been seized by invaders, and parcelled out among their followers. Later they have been confiscated for religious or political reasons, and similarly distributed. Honest men, useful men, genuine noblemen, may now be the innocent possessors of this wealth – but they have inherited with it the grave – the terrible responsibility of using it for the benefit of the heirs of those from whom it was taken, or those to whom it now justly belongs. All this wealth, all the culture it has given, all the power and prestige which belongs to its possession, must be used for the good of the people whose labour now, from year to year, gives all value to the land, and pays all interests and dividends on capital.

Wealth, recently acquired, is the sign of talent, energy, greed, craftiness, perhaps of utter selfishness and crime. A millionaire may be a clever and successful gambler, whose success has impoverished thousands. Not much can be said of an Aristocracy of financiers, speculators, or of men in any kind of business who merely make money. The worship of wealth, no matter how acquired, is one of the basest of human infirmities. The fact that money will buy a church living, a seat in Parliament, admission to good society, an honourable matrimonial alliance, is a very shameful one. A purse-proud Aristocracy is very despicable – but those who are ready to sell themselves for gold are more to be despised than those who are ready to buy them. The pride of wealth is base, the worship of wealth is contemptible.

Honour to whom honour is due. Render unto Caesar the things that are Caesar's. The true aristocracy – the best men and the best women of the nation – are honourable and right honourable. All worth, all merit, all excellence is worthy of honour and reward. Good men and good women on earth, and saints in heaven, have a just claim upon our reverence. It is a virtue to appreciate virtue, honourable to honour it. If we cannot live a true life, it is something to say amen to it – something to admire it and glorify it. We seek what we love, we emulate what we admire. Let us cherish then every atom of genuine aristocracy, of real excellence, we have among us, and every sign, and fragment, and relic of it. Paeans to the immortal living and the immortal dead.

The true aristocrat is an honest man – the noblest work of God; a good man, full of kindness and charity; a just man, rendering unto every one according to his works; a benevolent man, seeking the good of all around him; a generous man, bestowing bounties with a liberal hand; a brave man, ready to defend the weak, and rescue the oppressed; a noble man, scorning everything selfish, and sordid, and base; a heroic man, fit to take the lead in every great enterprise, and give fortune and life itself in the service of humanity. The higher we can place such men, and the more power we entrust to them, the better for all of us. We want such men to lead us onward and upward, and inspire us with their own purity and devotion.

RELIGION

All good behaviour is based upon religion, or the relation which exists between God and man, and between each man and his fellow-creatures. True religion is therefore the perfection of manners and morals.

Essentially, religion is the love of God; but the manifestation of that love is in the love of our neighbour, and the performance of all our social duties. The practical side of religion is morality. Faith is the spring of good works; good works are the manifestation of faith.

To quarrel about religion is irreligious – a violation of that charity which is its essence and supreme grace. Every form of religion has something of truth and goodness. Any religion is better than none. It is an aspiration to a higher and purer life – a recognition, however imperfect, of the relations of men to each other, and to the Father of All.

There being only one God, there can be but one true religion. All men have the same relation to God, and the same duties to their fellow men.

Differences in religion come of ignorance and pride or self-will. The ignorant need to be instructed by the wise; but the selfish are essentially irreligious and wicked. They have not the disposition or will to be right. They pervert the faith, as they would the multiplication table, to gratify selfishness, pride, vain glory, injustice, inequity, un-righteousness. Those who love the truth come to it sooner or later. Unselfish goodwill leads straight on to all truth and all goodness.

Of many ways, there must be a straightest and best way; of many forms, the highest and purest form; and it is that we have to seek. If two modes of religion differ, one must be better than the other. We need the best. If two sects teach opposite doctrines, both may be wrong, but one must be. Of twenty or a hundred varying creeds, only one can possibly be right.

Religious differences are deplorable difficulties in politics, in education, in society. How can two walk together unless they be agreed? Variations in religious faith separate wives from husbands, children from parents; prevent or destroy friendships; divide society into repellent castes and hostile camps; and hinder all united and harmonious action.

Mahomed founded his great, strange empire on compulsory conformity. For ages Christians considered heresy a crime against the State, to be punished, repressed, and stamped out. Dungeon and sword, torture, gibbet and stake, cold steel and hot fire, have been used in this country, as in others, by Catholics against Protestants, by Protestants against Catholics, as each had the political power. The State strove to keep its unity, as an army does to maintain its discipline. Political animosities were intensified by religious zeal; but religion had small part in these barbarous persecutions. It was the love of power, and not the love of God, that prompted the burning of heretics in Spain, the atrocities of Catholics and Huguenots in France, and the persecutions under Henry VIII., Edward VI., Mary, Elizabeth, and Cromwell. Religion has been a pretext and excuse for acts of human pride, selfishness, and cruelty. All fanaticism has the elements of pride and self-will, and the lack of the very core and essence of religion – Charity.

The Bible exhorts, entreats, commands the most perfect unity of faith, and the most perfect charity of feeling. There can of course be but one Church, the mystical body of Christ, and pillar and ground of truth. There can be but one faith, which all were exhorted to hold in perfect unity. Christ could not have taught two inconsistent and opposing doctrines, nor founded two churches opposed to each other. The unity of church and faith are logical necessities; and such unity seems to be absolutely necessary to all true political and social organisation – to all right progress and real prosperity and happiness.

It seems to me that every unprejudiced person must see that if there is any true religion, there can be but one; if there is any Church, only one is possible; and that the unity of Christendom is the condition of its power and progress.

What then is our duty? Evidently to be patient and charitable toward all from whom we differ, and earnestly seek to know and to do the right. The way to unity is for all to approach some common standard. Things which are equal to the same thing are equal to each other. Those who love the same things love each other. The higher the love the higher the unity it inspires. When men perfectly love God they will perfectly love one another.

If men could lay aside all prejudices, all opinions of others, and, in the simple love of truth, read the gospels and epistles of the New Testament, as one might read them for the first time, with no kind of prepossessions, I believe they would see their way more clearly than they can in the mists of the necessary errors of conflicting sects. But a red light makes all things red; a blue light colours the whole landscape blue. No man can see the truth who first puts on spectacles of error.

The essential thing is purity of intention; a wish and a will to be right and to do right – to deal justly, to love mercy, to walk humbly before God. This is the highest manhood and the true religion.

In religion, each point of belief includes all others. The first section of the Apostle's creed – 'I believe in God the Father Almighty', holds all the rest; as does the 'Our Father who art in Heaven' contain all the petitions which follow. So 'Love is the fulfilling of the law.' The truths of religion are self-evident, its mysteries inconceivable: we are compelled to believe the truths, and these require our assent to mysteries which do not contradict, but transcend our reason. No truth is unreasonable, but many facts in nature, even, are utterly incomprehensible. We understand nothing of the forces of cohesion, repulsion, gravitation. We observe phenomena, but all causes are mysteries. They exist and act notwithstanding, and we believe in them, though we cannot comprehend them. We really know no more of what we call the natural, than we do of what we call the supernatural; but we believe in both. The adaptations of man to the supernatural – to the facts of God and Immortality – are as evident to our minds as are our adaptations to the world around us. Take God and Immortality from man, and what we have left is so little, and so little worth, that life can scarcely be said to have motives, objects, or value. Thus religion is the basis of virtue – the crown and glory of manhood.

Miscellaneous Maxims

It may be thought that I have dealt too much with the principles of behaviour, and too little with rules of practice. But principles come into acts. Being manifests itself in doing. Love and hate, and all passions, emotions, sentiments, and thoughts find their natural expression.

The Bible is full of maxims of morals and conduct, and examples of the highest dignity and virtue. There is no better manual of politeness. We cannot imagine our highest models of the Christian life as other than perfect gentlemen and ladies – as persons whom we may well imitate in the smallest items of conduct.

The highest grace is charity. Charity is love to God and man. Whatever violates that love is contrary to religion and morals. To love nature is to love the Author of nature. We love and serve God in his humanity.

The motive is the essential thing in all our conduct. God takes the will for the deed. With Him what we wish to do, what we try to do, is done.

The true order of life is first use, then beauty; but use and beauty are never far apart. The most useful things in nature are the most beautiful. The finest forms of men and animals for strength and agility are the most elegant and graceful.

We should so order our lives as to make the most of them, wasting no time, no strength, no thought. Needs are pressing, and life is short. We must economise time by order, and force by doing the best work.

Never hurry. Whatever is worth doing at all, is worth doing well. Plan everything, and work to the plan. Carry conscience into every act of life. In eating a meal, consider what is best for you, and how much; and do not vary in one or the other.

Learn what is meant by the maxim: 'Whether ye eat or drink, or whatsoever ye do, do all to the glory of God.' The glory of God is inseparable from, and solely known to us in, the highest good of His creatures.

Learn to tolerate criticism, and profit by it. We should no more resent another's opinion of our conduct than our own. We are never to needlessly impute bad motives to the censures of others. Whether censure is intended for our good or not, we should disarm the critic by our thanks, and turn the criticism to good account. An artist shows his picture, and invites people to point out its faults; which, if he can see, he can mend. We should calmly do the same as to all our conduct. He who can bear to be told of his faults, that he may mend them, is well on the way to the highest excellence.

Anger dwells in the bosom of fools. There is a just or righteous indignation; but its expression must be self-possessed, calm, charitable. Whatever the provocation we receive, we must rule our own spirits, and not give place to wrath – not be beside ourselves. Whatever we may owe to others, we owe this to ourselves. An angry man is a lunatic. All violence of temper is of the nature of insanity. We must gain and keep self-control, as the first condition of right conduct.

Silence is sometimes golden. Better silence than senseless gabble. Better silence than replies that irritate and wound. People who would never descend to the vulgarity of a blow are peevish, nagging, sarcastic, rude, insolent, abusive in speech. Their words wound like blows, or pierce like sharp spears. Words vex, annoy, irritate, poison, and sometimes kill. Men who are taken before the magistrates for wife-beating are not the worst of brutes. 'A soft answer turneth away wrath, but grievous words stir up anger.'

The maxim of a gentleman is '*suaviter in modo: fortiter in re.*' He should be as gentle, suave, courteous in manner, as he is firm and energetic in all right actions. He must do his duty; but he need not jostle against or run over people in doing it. Roughness, brusqueness, incivility, are no part of duty-doing. If a man is obliged even to take the life of another, in the discharge of his duty, he should do it with perfect kindness and courtesy. Resolutely do the right – the highest and best right – and habit will make it easy, and custom and conscience will make it delightful.

Habit governs mind and morals as well as nerves and muscles. We form habits of truth and honesty, of benevolence and religion. All kinds of good behaviour can be learned, and by persevering repetition made habitual. Thus polite, attentive, graceful, and gracious manners become involuntary, and part and parcel of our life.

All the best part of education is learning how to behave. Reading, writing, arithmetic, and all the sciences, can be picked up at odd hours anywhere.

Inconsiderate people ask – How can we know what is true, and right, and best, when there are such wide differences of opinion? But morals are as certain as geometry. Right and wrong are as different as a circle and a square. No man sees white as black, or a crooked thing as straight.

As a gardener every day clears away weeds, and cultivates plants and flowers, so a man should every day correct faults, and improve his mind and manners. The best work of every life is self-culture first, and then, and chiefly by that means, help in the culture of others.

The one right way of getting into society is to qualify one's self to be its charm and ornament.

No distinctions of rank can do away with the respect due from youth to age, or the reverence man owes to woman.

The protection of a woman from the first encroachments of impudent familiarity is a prudent reserve of manner toward every man capable of such conduct. When it occurs it should be instantly checked by the indignant surprise it naturally excites.

Fussiness, dressiness, display of riches, titles, or distinctions of any kind, are 'snobbish' vulgarities. The one corrective is modesty. All snobbery is assumption. Every kind of attempt at display has in it selfishness and vulgarity. The law of perfect manners is simplicity and forgetfulness of self.

Simplicity of language is more truly elegant than any laboured floridness of speech. The best speakers and writers use the most familiar words. High flown expressions are as pretentious as inappropriate displays of dress and ornament.

Virtues may become vices by excess. Excess of order, neatness, cleanliness, prudence, may become annoying, ridiculous, and even insane. Fastidiousness, scruples, prudery, timidity, are faults of character and manners. We must accommodate ourselves to the world as we find it, and make it better as we can.

Gossip and scandal are the vices of little minds and bad hearts. The rule of law should be the rule of society – everyone should be considered innocent until proved guilty. Charity hopeth all things. Society is neutral ground where all quarrels cease. People leave swords and pistols at home – they should leave their tempers at home also. Adapt your manners to your company. When in Rome, do as the Romans do. This rule has its limits, but it is best to conform, as far as possible, to the manners of the country or society we are in. If people do not wear gloves, take yours off.' If they all eat from one dish with their fingers, what can you do but follow their example?

We have two words which express what no gentleman and no lady should be – 'fast' and 'slow'. We are offended with the fast, and bored with the slow. The fast is excessive, pretentious, imprudent, or impudent. Fast people are bold or slangy in conversation, eccentric in dress and manners, extravagant, and on the verge of indecorum. Slow people are tiresome.

Enter the tent of an Arab, and when you have eaten with him, you are safe in his protection – safe if you have been his bitterest foe. But in civilisation, the man who asks you to drink or to dine, may be plotting to swindle you.

Never press people unduly to eat, or drink, or stay. True politeness consists in putting people at their ease, and giving them all possible freedom; but a fussy ceremoniousness is always impertinent.

Never intrude on people at their meals. Never presume to take a seat near your most intimate friend at a public table, or in an eating house, without a decided invitation. Never sit so as to see people who are eating, unless requested to do so. Carefully avoid intrusions at all times, and particularly at meal times.

True politeness is cosmopolitan. It goes like sunshine around the globe. Like the ocean, it encloses all continents. Like the atmosphere, it envelopes all humanity. There is nothing narrow or sectional in any great thought or love. All true and truly noble things are universal.

Whatever your own private opinions or inclinations may be, a certain regard is always to be paid to the opinions of others.

If music of a Sunday evening offends your neighbours within hearing, or even those who pass in the street, it had better be dispensed with. There can be no complete independence or individuality in this respect, unless you can isolate yourself from public observation.

At church, a quiet, serious deportment; an absence of all irreverence, gaiety, whisperings; a courteous attention to the preacher and the service, are absolute requisites. You should not loll, nor yawn, nor sleep, nor do anything to annoy preacher or congregation. The church is no place for exhibitions of connubial affection, nor flirtations, courtships, or coquetries; nor for ordinary reading or business.

The way to make friendships lasting and happy, is never to violate the principles of courtesy or good breeding with those you call your friends. They are entitled to as good treatment, to say the least, as other people – yet they often get the worst. Good society is an entertainment, to which good behaviour is a ticket of admission.

It is a crime to murder language; it is cruel to torture the ears of our neighbours; and the good opinion of those around us is worth taking a little pains for.

Endeavour to acquire and use, as round, smooth, sweet, solid and pure a tone as is possible to you. Avoid the nasal twang or whine; it is odious. Avoid the flat tone; it is flat. Avoid the guttural, the husky, the rough, the sharp, the dry, the cold; for all these terms characterise tones of the voice itself, and aside from its modulations.

Articulate clearly, and with entire distinctness, then, every word you have to speak. A clear articulation makes up for lack of force. Even deaf people can understand better those who speak distinctly, than those who only speak loud. Clear articulation makes speech like a beautiful engraving, in which every line is distinct, while the careless and blundering manner of many speakers is like a blurred and defaced copy, in which every outline is lost.

A musician will practice ten hours a day, for five or ten years, to thoroughly master his art and instrument. Is it not worth as much effort to become a good writer; by which means a retired student and even a feeble woman may sometimes move the world of mind, and shape the destinies of nations?

In regard to conversation, it is a capital rule, though seldom followed, not to speak, unless you have something to say. Do what demands the doing is a great rule of life. Let supply be governed by demand. Speak what asks to be said; write what wishes to be written.

Every letter requiring an answer should be immediately attended to, particularly if on business. To not answer when written to, is the same kind of rudeness as not to speak when spoken to. In either case there may be a good reason for silence.

In a friendly correspondence, the first letter should be answered as soon as received; but the second should be delayed the same interval as that taken by the first writer, who in this way regulates the frequency of the correspondence. This is a good rule among equals; but where a gentleman writes to a lady, he can hardly delay an immediate answer, unless at her own request.

Where a letter is long, or important; where there are matters to be attended to, or subjects requiring consideration – a brief note should be sent at once, acknowledging the receipt of the letter, and promising a fuller answer.

In giving, we must give nobly, and often a very little makes all the difference. The man is a 'perfect gentleman' who gives half-a-crown when, if he gave two shillings, he would be thought and called a sneak. Give a little more than is expected, as the overplus tells more in the feelings and opinions of others than all the rest. Beware of a reputation for stinginess; and if you have any tendency in this direction, make a principle of guarding against the manifestation of so odious and ungentlemanly a vice.

It is our right to gather useful and beautiful things around us, if we can do so honestly – that is, without any violation of the rights of others. To be honestly rich, to be rich with a full recognition of the rights of others, is noble, and praiseworthy in all respects. Everyone has the right to acquire, by just and equitable means, land, a home of beauty, food, clothing, books, pictures, all that contribute to the necessaries, the real enjoyments, and true luxuries of life.

To gather riches in grasping avarice and greed for gain, in grinding the face of the poor, in spoliation and plunder of any kind, whether on a large or small scale, and by whatever trick or chicane of finance, commerce, or legalised robbery, is contrary to justice, and so unworthy of a gentleman.

No gentleman or lady can be niggard, stingy, selfish, and mean. Avarice is one of the most ungentlemanly vices, as it is opposed to the two noble virtues of justice and generosity.

Habitually regard the rights of others. You cannot come into the presence of another but there arises this question of rights. Guard your own from unscrupulous and wanton violation, but be still more careful not to trespass upon those of others. Courteously grant a little more than justice requires. Turn out a little more than half way. Nothing is lost by courtesy. The sentiment of justice, though often perverted and lost sight of, still rules humanity. The very organ grinder knows he can trust it, and that, if you listen to his music, you will give him your penny in return.

When you borrow money, if but a sixpence, pay it with scrupulous punctuality. There is a delicacy in these matters that cannot be violated. Borrow as seldom as possible; lend cheerfully, courteously, when you can; and refuse firmly where the loan is too much or the risk too great. Offer your purse as freely as you do any other civility, where it may be needed. Those best entitled to such assistance, are often the last to ask, or the most unwilling to accept it.

Never treat a debtor rudely. The most despicable insolence is that of the purse. If a man cannot pay, you gain nothing by insult or harsh treatment; if unwilling to pay, he feels justified in his refusal by your bad manners. The creditor who abuses or insults a debtor, really loses his claim to the money, for the insult should be considered an offset.

Avoid all indebtedness if possible; but if you must owe, let it be to few persons, and in large amounts, rather than small ones. Pay all little personal matters, and the needy, and owe those who can afford to wait, and whom you can compensate.

It is often better to go to a pawnbroker or a man who makes a business of lending, than borrow money of an acquaintance; it is seldom, indeed, that one can properly borrow of an acquaintance, unless a loan is voluntarily offered. As a matter of principle, no form ought to be customary or obligatory, which may in some cases be disagreeable. In some countries kissing is the common salutation of both sexes. According to the French code, a woman gives her hand to a gentleman to kiss, her cheek to her friends, but scrupulously keeps her lips for her lover. To allow one she did not love to kiss her on her lips, would be an outrage on the delicacy of sentiment.

A true gentleman will do anything proper for him to do. He can soil his hands or use his muscles when there is occasion. The truest gentleman is more likely to carry home a market-basket or a parcel, or to wheel a barrow through the street, than many a conceited little snob of a shop-boy.

Society has no measure of character. It demands, therefore, a certain style, dress, manner, and reputation, as the best guarantees it can have.

The clergyman who should reveal the confidences of a parishioner; the physician or surgeon who should betray the secret of some malady or operation; the lawyer who should gossip of the affairs of his client, would deserve universal execration; so does any person who betrays confidences or even accidental discoveries of a similar character.

When a misfortune has occurred, or a crime has been committed, people seem to act as if it were desirable, by the utmost publicity, to aggravate the evil; when the first impulse with everyone should be to remedy, to conceal, if publicity be undesirable, and to prevent future evils of a similar character. Where the pride of a family, the reputation of a woman for virtue, or a man for honesty, are threatened, those who raise a hue-and-cry are something worse than the wolves who fall upon and devour a wounded companion.

Never boast of any service you have rendered another: perhaps a good general rule, covering all particulars, would be never to boast at all.

Never ridicule the country, religion, or love of any one. It is well to remember, that it was only the little incident of being born in one place rather than another, that has prevented you from being a Turk, or Chinaman, or whatever you may happen not to like.

Husband and wife are like two persons in the cabin of the same ship: bound to make the voyage together. But in society they are to forget each other – they are one, the husband is to the wife another self – but she must forget herself.

Those who are ready to believe evil of others judge them out of a consciousness of their own habitual desires; and this may be, and often is, a false judgment.

The man who thinks another will commit any immorality, because he has the opportunity, judges himself with a terrible judgment, because he judges another out of his own heart. Humanity and religion demand that we exercise the charity of attributing the best motives rather than the worst; and a charitable judgment, while it is humane to others, is favourable to ourselves. Every good feeling, and every good action, meet with a sure and abundant reward, if only in the consciousness of right endeavour.

'Fear God; honour the king.' We fear most to offend those whom we should most love: then 'perfect love casteth out fear.' In the love of perfect charity we love God supremely, and all creatures in him and for his sake. We honour the king as the representative of justice and order; and honour all their ministers, down to the common soldier and police constable.

True life is in order – law, authority, obedience. It is well to understand, so as to give a wise obedience to an orderly authority; but obedience, even to unwise command, is the first element of order.

We stumble, and learn to walk. Our blunders educate us. In the end, every man works out his own destiny.